Hea

'Melvin Banks knows a God who is active through words, works and wonders . . . I recommend this book. It will encourage and stimulate many to believe in all that our God is doing today'

Clive Calver

'Fascinating . . . thrilling and encouraging . . .'

Rev Noel Procter
(Anglican Chaplain, H.M. Prison, Strangeways, Manchester).

'Genuine . . . real miracle cures . . . Rev Banks works through the greater doctor Jesus Christ . . .'

Dr Q. M. Adams, M.R.C.P., L.R.C.S., M.F.Hom.
(former Harley Street Consultant).

'A great account . . . every person should read this . . .'

Dr Fred Roberts
(Christian Centre, Durban, S. Africa, with 4,000 affiliate members).

'A tremendous, inspiring account of Christ's power today . . .'

Rev John Coleman
(leading pastor in New Zealand).

Healing Secrets

Melvin Banks

with

David Lee

Marshall Morgan and Scott
Marshall Pickering
3 Beggarwood Lane, Basingstoke, Hants RG23 7LP, UK

First published in 1986 by Marshall Morgan and Scott (Publications) Ltd
Part of the Marshall Pickering Holdings Group
A subsidiary of the Zondervan Corporation

Reprinted : Impression number
87 88 89 90 : 10 9 8 7 6 5 4 3 2

ISBN: 0 551 01356 7

Text set in Plantin by Brian Robinson, Buckingham
Printed in Great Britain by Hazell Watson & Viney Limited,
Member of the BPCC Group, Aylesbury, Bucks

I once again dedicate this book to the only one most worthy, to the most marvellous girl a man could have as a partner, my beloved wife Lilian. Also to my faithful mother, whose prayers have been such a power in this ministry over the past thirty years.

Note on cover illustration:
The cover of this book shows a typical front page newspaper shot of someone who has discovered that the Healing Secrets of God work! It is merely one of 400 reports which have appeared in national and provincial newspapers, and have been collected by the Revd. Banks and his team over a period of 21 years.

Contents

Acknowledgements

To my excellent team, who give me such valuable back-up and inspiration in this great work. I think particularly of Brian Hilliard, Keith Simons, Chris Morton, Maurice and Christine Cowling, Peter Cross, Trevor Slattery, Spiro Katchis, Jean and Norman Clark, Ron Pagan, Philip and Paul Banks and Allan and Shirley Simons. Above all I acknowledge the help of many ordinary, humble 'disciples' and members of the Assemblies of God, Christian Fellowships, House Churches and many other churches and fellowships, who have all worked together with us in making known the Healing Secrets of Christ to our generation.

It is good for the brethren to dwell together in unity . . .

—Psalm 133:1

Ask me, and I will tell you some remarkable secrets.

—Jeremiah 33:3 (Living Bible)

1: It Works

An argument is always at the mercy of an experience.
Billy Sunday

On *Channel Four* recently I saw a discussion on Christian healing. It was a remarkable discussion because it began by discounting all miraculous healing as hysteria and hearsay. The presenters didn't even waste any time talking about it: they simply said, 'Well, we know that's all nonsense so let's get on to the real issue – the behaviour of Christians in the medical profession . . . .'

This surprised me, to say the least! It was like being a foundry worker and having someone tell you that there's no such thing as iron. If miracles were as rare as luminous black butterflies in Iceland, I could understand someone doubting the good faith of people who claim to have seen them. But miracles aren't rare. They're not even restricted to certain kinds of healing that might just reasonably be explained by some other theory, like mind over matter. Take this example.

A lot of my work recently has been overseas, in poor countries where missions have to be supported by the generosity of Christians at home. The pastors and congregations are always extremely, even sacrificially kind; but I still have to watch my spending pretty closely to make sure I don't run out of cash. On a trip like this I woke up one morning on a hard bed in a bare room and realised I was getting short – in travellers' cheques and local currency I had seventy-six dollars. I put the notes back in my wallet and committed the matter to God in prayer. I received no more money over the next ten days, and in fact had to spend some on meals out, so it was with great surprise that I found at the next count I had fifty dollars more than I'd had the last time. I recounted. There was no doubt about it – fifty dollars extra.

Since I kept my wallet locked up in my case there was no possibility of anyone but me gaining access to it. Had I simply forgotten how much I had? To make certain I wrote down the figure on a piece of paper and locked it up in the case with the money. But I hadn't forgotten – when I counted again a week later I had more money still. Not that I was complaining, since my financial needs, which had earlier been the source of some anxiety, were now being amply met.

Eventually the crusade came to an end and the time came for me to change all my remaining credit into English currency. I had worked out how much I needed and it coincided exactly with the amount I had to exchange. I watched the bank teller count it out.

'That should give me fifteen pounds.'

'Fifteen pounds and three pence,' she said, pushing the notes over the counter. 'The exchange rate rose this morning. Have a good flight.'

I pocketed the money and walked out, only to be called back half a minute later by another bank clerk.

'There's been a mistake.'

'Did she give me too much?'

'No, you gave *her* too much.'

The teller was holding out a note. I took it, and immediately pushed it back at her.

'This is a hundred dollars!'

'It was in the currency you gave me, Sir.'

'Are you sure?'

At my insistence she counted the money twice more, and each time there were a hundred dollars left over.

'Well,' I said, feeling a bit foolish, 'I suppose I'd better take it.'

After a long flight I arrived at Heathrow and boarded the coach for Wiltshire. There wasn't much to do – there never is on coaches – so I turned out my pockets and counted the coins. Excluding the hundred dollars (which I set aside for mission funds) eight weeks' crusading had left me with precisely forty pence. If it hadn't been for God's miraculous provision of cash half way through the journey I wouldn't even have had that. But being penniless didn't bother me, because in spiritual terms I was rich beyond measure. I had seen five thousand people converted and eleven thousand prayed for, almost eighty per cent of whom in some areas had testified to definite healing. What is money in a business that runs on miracles? Whose profits are assessed in terms of souls saved, churches founded, men and women filled with the Holy Spirit?

Those television presenters, I suppose, would have said I was kidding myself. But for me there is no ambiguity. In the end all businessmen have to face up to the cold facts of the balance sheet; and I would have left the miracle ministry a long time ago if I didn't know for sure that it *works*. And if that is true, then as Peter and John said to the Jewish elders, 'We cannot but speak the things which we have seen and heard' (Acts. 4:20). The purpose of this book, then, is not to prove divine healing: it does not need to be proved. What I want to do is examine the secrets of the healing ministry, the *why* and *how* of healing that you need to be in on whether you're receiving healing or ministering it. Understanding the treatment is, after all, very useful for a patient and absolutely essential for the doctor . . . .

But that is jumping the gun. In the medical world successful treatment depends first of all on a sound understanding of the disease. So I begin *Healing Secrets* by asking a question – Why is healing necessary at all?

2: Big Trouble

Though fallen creatures and inheritors of Adam's curse . . . we may aspire to participate in the purposes of God.

Malcolm Muggeridge

A word we all use a good deal nowadays is *problem*. It is an interesting word because it combines our awareness of difficulties with a resolute faith in our ability to tackle them. Football hooliganism is a *problem*, but we feel it can be contained if the right measures are taken against it; cancer is a *problem* – but it comforts us immensely to think of all those scientists beavering away in search of a cure. In one way solving problems is what human life is all about; as H. G. Wells pointed out, 'If a man had no difficulties or troubles in life, what on earth would he do with himself?'

Most of the time, with a bit of help from the media, we can persuade ourselves that problems are solvable. After all, the people at the BBC look so perpetually cheerful that there really *must* be a lot of us left who can cope with divorces, wrinkles and baldness and not let the smile slip from our faces. And when the hero of this or that drama series emerges from the casualty unit after a horrendous crash in the Swiss Alps, it's remarkable just how *perfect* a job those plastic surgeons have made of restoring his good looks. In the world of television every game show has a winner, every criminal is tracked down. Even the weathermen look happy, goodness knows why.

But come the end of the evening we have to switch off the set (the licence needs renewing) and fiddle around in the kitchen cabinet trying to find the sleeping pills (they ran out yesterday); lock the doors on the house that's already been mortgaged for ten years, get undressed in the bathroom that the kids half-wrecked before they went to the disco, and finally climb into bed knowing that in six hours' time the alarm will summon us to another day of soul-destroying work where the pay almost, but not quite, keeps up with the rate of inflation. At that moment it may occur to us that problems, however minor in themselves, are able to overwhelm us by their sheer weight of numbers. If only the wife's father hadn't had his stroke; if only the car hadn't given out before its MOT; if only the kids would behave. It seems to go on and on and on and well, frankly, it's all a bit much.

Add to that the comprehensive threat of nuclear war and life can get pretty depressing. In fact depression – the inability to hold up under the stresses that life imposes on us – has in the twentieth century become a problem in its own right. Fortunately most of us experience it only occasionally, but even when we are keeping on top of things we are aware of the backdrop of difficulties against which our private and national life is played out. Some of these, of course, are the healthy challenges of perfecting our performance in athletics, sport and science; but more often they constitute a vague sense that all is not well with the world and that in our struggle to put it right the odds are stacked heavily against us.

At the centre of this is something that the Bible calls *darkness*. It is a metaphorical term referring to the power and influence of Satan, perhaps chosen in the first place because physical darkness brings with it a sense of danger and vulnerability. Darkness stands for evil, malevolence and ignorance, over and against which Christ brings light and truth. It is able to influence the minds of those who refuse to believe in Christ (2 Cor. 4:5) and characterises their actions (Eph. 6:12). It is also symbolic of judgment and final damnation, since it was one of the plagues God brought upon Egypt and is clearly cited as a feature of hell – more often in fact than the traditional flames.

The metaphor has been picked up repeatedly by writers

and novelists and most recently by film-makers. Many readers will be familiar with William Golding's *Lord of the Flies* in which the unfortunate Simon looks into the spiked pig's head to find 'a blackness within . . . a blackness that spread . . . ', or with J. R. R. Tolkein's *Lord of the Rings* and its constant linking of the theme of darkness with evil and confusion. The same concept applied to a different medium determines the black costume of the infamous Darth Vador in the *Star Wars* series.

Examples could be multiplied. The important thing to realise is that the theme of darkness survives in books and music and films because its meaning is instantly recognisable to us. Something instinctive in us gets the adrenalin moving when we are alone at night. But not only that: the presence of the physical darkness that is a simple product of the earth's spinning around the sun also seems to precipitate the other, spiritual darkness. During a recent power workers' strike in New York a large area of the city was blacked out for an entire night. It gave rise to the worse wave of crime–of mugging, looting and rape–that the police force had ever had to cope with: one officer described it later as 'all hell let loose'. An apt phrase; but also ironic, since many of those who took part in the crime were previously honest, law-abiding citizens.

The episode presses home the Bible's point that 'all have sinned, and come short of the glory of God' (Rom. 3.23). And it is remarkable how often thinkers who profess no Christian faith at all manage to back this up. The humanist philosopher C. M. Joad said that 'evil is an epidemic in man,' and further, that 'the doctrine of original sin expresses a deep insight into human nature.' W. Somerset Maugham observed 'in morals and in character how similar all men are.' And even the Greek philosopher Aristotle came to the conclusion that 'there is no good in mankind.' The fact is, alongside our rather faint desire to do good there lies a stronger propensity to do evil. Paul the Apostle pinpointed it exactly when he admitted, 'The good that I would I do not: but the evil that I would not, that I do' (Rom. 7:19).

There are no two ways about it that this negative twist in man's nature is impairing and destructive both of ourselves and of the others we mix with. It is, to put it succinctly, a *deviation*.

Although Mark Twain once defined man as 'the only animal who blushes when he is guilty' a feeling of guilt is not always the consequence of deviation in the human personality; or at least the guilt is very carefully suppressed. A splendid example of this was provided for me recently by a woman who at the end of a week's crusade told me in a strong Oxford accent how impressed she was with all she had seen. Only one thing rankled with her, and when I asked her what it was she replied, 'I did not like you talking about my sins every night.' It is certainly a fact that too much attention paid to our shortcomings is something that makes all of us a bit uncomfortable. When, for instance, was the last time you justified some action or attitude by saying, 'Well, I'm no worse than anyone else!'

The dogged persistence of this deviation, its tendency to cling to us whatever we do, may explain our attempts to reconcile ourselves to it. Usually these take the form of verbal cosmetics: finding other names that make it sound a bit better than it really is. Politicians, of course, are past masters of this technique, as you will soon find out if you hear a Cabinet Minister being interviewed on the latest downturn in the economy. But to some extent or another we all do it. 'It's only fair to tell people the truth,' we say, after bowling someone over with a torrent of pretty prejudice; or, 'I had a little accident last night,' meaning we were blind drunk and ran the car into a lamp post. And, of course, what we do as individuals our society does at a wider scale. Pornography becomes 'adult entertainment'; homosexuals, the 'gay community'; sin and deviation, 'human nature'.

That way we are able to live with it and in the very worst instances actually dignify it – a strange reversal given the judgment of the Bible which, in spite of themselves, the intellectual movements of our century have tended to confirm. In the words of Paul, men are 'without Christ, being aliens from the commonwealth of Israel, and strangers from the covenants of promise, having no hope, and without God in the world . . . ' (Eph. 2:12). Ths kind of statement is customarily rejected as old fashioned and irrelevant, but in fact it points to the only key with which we may unlock our self-styled prison. C. S. Lewis emphasises that however unpopular it may seem, 'The recovery of the old sense of sin is essential.' Since God addresses his gospel to those who admit their sin, it stands to reason that those who will not admit it 'lack the first condition for understanding what he is talking about.' The man who insists he is well will never be persuaded to consult a doctor.

Clearly this inconsistency cannot go unnoticed, and in fact it shows itself in a range of symptoms that, for the sake of neatness, we will call *dissatisfaction.* At its most basic this is just what the word suggests – the feeling that all of us have had at some time or other (and some of us have all the time) that we're not getting all we could out of life. Sometimes we are tempted to think we've been given a downright rotten deal; and that's not surprising when you think that our particular culture runs on a market economy. In the first place this is all very good because it enables us to obtain the basic commodities we need: food, clothes and heat. But it isn't long before someone comes along with the bright idea of embellishing those commodities; so the housewife in the local supermarket, who used to buy Mush Flakes, now has the choice of buying Mush Flakes fortified with iron. Any conscientious housewife will know that iron is a good thing – even in Mush Flakes – so she gets them. Encouraged by his success the producer comes up with a third option: Mush Flakes fortified with iron and vitamins, with a fluoride component (approved by dentists), extra fibre, and the offer of a free plastic model of Superman on receipt of three Mush Flakes packet tops. He also pushes up the price, proof (if proof were needed) that Mush Flakes Mk. 3 is the most superior product ever to hit the cereal bowl. Of course they're not; but they succeed because the manufacturer has grasped the principle that people will buy not just what they need, but what they think they need, and while the former is a more or less fixed list of items the latter can be extended at will by means of clever advertising.

The result is we are never satisfied. There's always a new fashion, a new gimmick for the car, a better lawnmower, a more effective aspirin, tastier lager or longer cigarette which until we have it will keep us from being fully respectable and completely content. Not that all new products are bad or unnecessary, or that the human desire for novelty is in itself an evil thing; since the economy runs on it we might think twice before trying to do away with it. The point is what it shows about our state of mind. Enough is never enough, because the space we are attempting to fill with all our material goods is always larger than the sum of the things we can share in. It was just the same for the Samaritan woman Jesus met at the well. A lifetime of acquiring commodities (in her case men) could not satisfy her desire, for the very simple reason that the desire had its roots in the *spiritual* realm. In that way she stood for us all. 'Whosoever drinketh of this water shall thirst again,' Christ said to her. 'But whosoever drinketh of the water that I shall give him shall never thirst' (John 4:13, 14).

That is why the proverb is true that says money cannot buy happiness. A woman who came to my meetings in Durham once said to me that since she had won the football pools she had quarrelled with her family and friends, and her life had sunk from relative contentment to abject misery. As soon as we get the thing we want, we find it's not the thing we want after all. So as George Bernard Shaw said, 'There are two tragedies in life. One is not to get everything you want and the other is to get it.' Always, complete satisfaction floats like a phantom just beyond our grasp. Like Alice approaching the Red Queen in the looking glass garden only to find herself walking in at the front door again, mankind sets out firmly to achieve total happiness through possessions, religion, drugs or love, and finds itself right back where it began.

What really happened in the Garden of Eden?

So: *darkness, deviation, dissatisfaction*: three aspects of the human condition that no doctor can treat. Not even a psychiatrist could treat them, because although they are experienced in the mind they have their roots in neither the body nor the mind, but in the spirit. So if we want to find out what this condition is, and how we caught it in the first place, we will have to go to the Bible.

The opening chapters of its first book, Genesis, give us a picture of man as he was originally created by God, and the beginning of something that has traditionally been called *original sin*. Contrary to popular belief original sin has nothing to do with either nakedness or apples, both of which as far as God is concerned may be indulged in freely provided (in the first case) that you are married, and (in the second) that the apples are ripe and you have paid for them. Nor was original sin simply a matter of man disobeying God and getting his wrist slapped. If we want something to compare it with we might take the case of a loving wife who returns home one day to find her husband in bed with another woman. When Adam ate the forbidden fruit he utterly and irrevocably betrayed God's trust in him, and spoiled his relationship with God in the same way that a marriage is spoiled by adultery. But there is more to it even than that, because the act of betrayal changed him, caused him in spiritual terms a fatal injury. C. S. Lewis explains it in *The Problem of Pain*:

> ' . . . the human spirit from being the master of human nature became a mere lodger in its own house, or even a prisoner . . . it had turned from God . . . and become its own idol, so that though it could still turn back to God, it could do so only by painful effort, and its inclination was selfward. Hence pride, ambition, the desire to be lovely in its own eyes and to depress and humiliate its rivals, envy and the restless search for more and more security, were now the attitudes that came easiest to it. It was not only a weak king over its own nature, but a bad one . . . (Adam

and Eve) wanted some corner of the universe in which they could say to God, 'This is our business, not yours,' but there is no such corner. . . . This condition was transmitted by heredity to all later generations . . . it was the emergence of a new kind of man – a new species, never made by God, had sinned itself into existence . . . '.

It is hard for us to understand just how completely monstrous this betrayal was. We often feel the same sympathy for Adam and Eve as we do for the elderly lady who, unable to bear the thought of being separated from her pet dog, hides the creature in her case while she travels on a plane. But ignorance is not innocence; if the dog has been in contact with rabies the ignorant act becomes the trigger for an epidemic and all the suffering that entails. Which is why, after man's fall, God took such swift and severe measures to contain it. He withdrew the spiritual power which had elevated man from his original, material being, and this allowed him to slip back into a curseful condition: 'Dust thou art, and unto dust shalt thou return' (Gen. 3:19). This was quenching the flames by starving them; weakening the foundation to prevent it supporting a greater edifice of sin and rebellion. For man it meant being released into the power of death. 'Wherefore,' says Paul, 'as by one man sin entered into the world . . . and so death passed upon all men' (Rom. 5:12).

This was first the foremost a spiritual death, but it had physical consequences. Not only man, but the whole of creation became susceptible to the process of degeneration and decay; whereas before the fall all things existed in harmony and illness was unknown, after it nothing could be found that would not in the course of time change, break down and disappear. Even the apparently permanent things, like the mountains and hills, were worn down under the patient attack of the elements, and man, who was created immortal, had his life span cut down to a meagre seven or eight decades, to be lived out in worry, pain and sickness. 'The days of our years are threescore years and ten . . . yet is their strength but labour and sorrow; for it is soon cut off, and we fly away' (Ps. 90:10).

By doing this God was not inflicting on mankind any evil of his own devising. He was rather loosening his hold a little so that man might have to endure the natural effect, in physical and spiritual terms, of his betrayal. This is important, because it means that in the business of healing we are not dealing with a small and exceptional disorder of an otherwise healthy creature, but with an entire spiritual condition. To put it very simply indeed, God allowed the original sin that produced darkness, deviation and dissatisfaction in the soul, to cause, for man's own good, sickness and death in the body—otherwise some far worse fate might have befallen us. Nonetheless it would not be true to say that sickness comes to us individually because God sends it. As John Alexander Dowie said, 'Sickness is the foul offspring of its mother sin and its father Satan.' Whatever part death and illness play in God's purpose for the human race they are not his own handiwork. In fact the spiritual and satanic roots of illness are often extremely clear.

The Bible gives several instances of physical illness being mediated by Satan or satanic agencies. Jesus described the woman with the crooked spine as 'a daughter of Abraham whom Satan hath bound, lo, these eighteen years' (Luke 13:16); and healing a boy who could neither hear no speak he addressed himself to an evil spirit: 'Thou deaf and dumb spirit, I charge thee, come out of him' (Mark 9:25). In the Old Testament an even clearer case arises in the story of Job. Seeking to prove that the holy man's devotion will last only as long as his material comforts Satan obtains permission to—among other things—bring him out in boils; which suggests that in some cases at least the direct causes of illness, be it virus, bacteria or organic disorders, are themselves subject to the influence of evil forces.

Other references make a strong connection between sickness and sin. 'Neither let us commit fornication,' Paul wrote to the Corinthian church, 'as some of them committed, and fell in one day three and twenty thousand' (1 Cor. 10:8). In the same letter he condemns the brazen impenitence with which the Corinthians were apt to take

Holy Communion, as 'For this cause many are weak and sickly among you, and many sleep' (1 Cor. 11:30). Leprosy appears more than once in the Old Testament as God's judgment against sin – on Miriam for her opposition to the prophet Moses (Num. 12:1–10) and on Gehazi, the servant of Elisha, for deception and greed (2 Kings 5:27). Peter, after emphasising the destructive effects of domestic strife, states the principle in its reverse form: 'For he that will love life, and see good days, let him refrain his tongue from evil, and his lips that they speak no guile' (1 Pet. 3:10).

In the realm of conventional medicine, although some doctors would still hesitate to use the word *spiritual*, it is almost a common place judgment nowadays that physical illness can have a root cause in the mind. The term *psychosomatic* was coined some time ago and does not mean, as it is sometimes taken to, that the patient is imagining his illness. On the contrary the trend has been to explain more and more physical disorders by factors that result from the lifestyle and attitude of the person who suffers them. The effect of stress on a heart condition is a well documented example. But other mental states – like fear and bitterness, which have a firm connection with the spiritual – are being recognised, even in secular medicine, as a cause of illness.

The Christian and sickness

The consequences of original sin are here for all of us, spiritually and physically. There is to be no easy return to innocence, no permanent happiness, no life immune from the rigours of degeneration even in an age of vitamin supplements and herbal medicine. To live a physical existence – to have a body – is to suffer illness and death. Only in the future millenial Kingdom of God is there any promise of release from the cycle; as John predicts in Revelation, 'God shall wipe away all tears from their eyes; and there shall be no more death, neither sorrow, nor crying, neither shall there be any more pain: for the former things are passed away' (Rev. 21.4).

The Christian, though, may feel he is entitled to be let off lightly. After all, although he lives in the body on this earth, he is in spirit already seated with Christ in heaven. In the world he may be, but he is not of it. He cannot be subject to the will of Satan in quite the same way as everybody else, since God watches over him to the extent of numbering every hair on his head. And the Old Testament gives ample assurance that faith and health are closely linked; as Hosea said, 'Come, and let us return unto the Lord; for he hath torn, and he will heal us; he hath smitten, and he will bind us up' (Hos. 6:1). What, then, is the right response when the Christian catches a cold, develops heart disease or contracts a cancer?

The first thing to do is recognise that God works in the life of a believer through illness. If nothing else, he may be giving a timely reminder that prudence about health and cleanliness, written into the Old Covenant, is not to be abandoned under the New. 'God did not promise that it would be unnecessary to observe the ordinary laws of health,' writes John Straton. 'Instead of this, He instructed His people in these elementary laws of health through Moses, His prophet, and gave to earth the benefit of the wisdom of heaven.' (*Divine Healing in Scripture and Life*). In view of this it is clear that the missionary who risks typhoid by drinking polluted water is placing himself in the hands of Satan.

But the Bible shows that God has spoken through illness for other reasons as well. In allowing leprosy to settle temporarily on Miriam (Num. 12:10) he wished to correct her behaviour, as a father might send a child to its room. With Job the purpose was exemplary, and it is interesting to note here that although the trial began as a proof of Job's faith, it was finally completed when Job and his three friends had reached a new and deeper understanding of God – which shows that there can be more to learn in illness than how quickly God puts it right. In two further instances from the Old Testament illness came as a retribution; first on Gehazi the servant of Elisha (2 Kings 5:27), then on King Jehoram, who after making a thoroughly good job of being evil was struck down with an agonising disease and 'departed with no one's regret' (2 Chron. 21:18–20).

The first two cases, Miriam and Job, form a pattern for the understanding of sickness in the Christian believer. Illness is allowed to develop for some specific purpose and withdrawn as soon as that purpose is fulfilled. This makes humble and repentant prayer an important priority for the Christian who is sick, and this may provide the key for a number of illnesses. On the other hand it has to be said that healing within the New Testament church was not assumed to be a matter of course. Paul mentions two friends for whom (we may conclude) prayer was not immediately effective: 'Trophimus . . . I left at Miletum sick' (2 Tim. 4:20) and Epaphroditus, who was 'sick nigh unto death' (Phil. 2:27).

It seems that as temptations afflict the soul, so illness afflicts the body; but of course this does not mean that sickness should be lamely submitted to any more than we should succumb to temptation. The implications for the Christian are spelled out by Paul in his letter to the Corinthians: 'Ye are bought with a price, therefore glorify God in your body, and in your spirit, which are God's' (1 Cor. 6:20). The believer strives to live in virtue and holiness by yielding to the indwelling presence of the Holy Spirit, and he glorifies God in his physical body as he yields to the divine life of Christ to maintain physical health and vigour. As John writes, 'For this purpose the Son of God was manifested, that he might destroy the works of the devil' (1 John 3:8). Being ill, of course, is not a sin, but it is the result of the devil's work and as such should be approached with firm, believing prayer. That way the Christian may discover fresh opportunities for repentance and the deepening of his walk with God; he may, like Job, find that peace lies in enduring the illness while God's greater purposes are worked out. Most often, however, he will find divine healing.

3: Divine Health

We must turn our attention from the visible disease and direct it upon man as a whole

Carl Jung

Our healing crusades usually get a good–if sensational–reaction from the press, and a while ago I saw a local newspaper article that both surprised and delighted me. It was written by a reporter I had met on my way to the platform at a meeting two days before. Hundreds of people had come together on this midsummer afternoon, more than could be comfortably accommodated even making use of the aisles and overflow rooms, and we were all practically frying in the heat. As I made my way down the main hall, shaking hands with the congregation as I generally do in the minutes before a service begins, I noticed a rather fat man struggling to his feet. His motions suggested someone had tied his ankles together, and this was causing some alarm to the ladies in the row behind him. But he soon righted himself, pulled out a notebook and called in my direction.

'Mr Banks!'

I turned. His glasses had just slipped off and he was busy pushing them back along his nose.

'Yes?'

'Mr Banks, would you please say–what is this divine healing?'

It was such a big question it took me a moment to think of an answer. Divine healing is, after all, the sort of thing it takes a book to explain properly, and even then you end up saying far less than the subject deserves. But this reporter who was standing a few feet away from me, the perspiration glistening on his forehead, pen poised on his pad, expected me to reply in seconds. 'It's God answering our prayers!' I said, quickly.

But his glasses had slipped again.

'Would you mind repeating that, Mr Banks?'

A couple of mornings later I was gratified to read in the local paper the headline: 'VICAR SAYS DIVINE HEALING IS GOD ANSWERING US–AND HE DOES!' Not that I am a vicar. But if God's healing power is going to get a good press I don't mind being mistaken for one. The reporter had clearly been impressed by what he saw, as are many of the reporters who come to cover the crusade meetings. That afternoon tremendous miracles had taken place: the deaf were hearing, the lame discarding their crutches or wheeling their chairs back home; and the reporter had told it just like it was. He had even got what for me was the ideal angle on his story–that healing comes completely and exclusively from God.

Of course there are a lot of other ways in which the sick can find some measure of healing or relief from their pains: drugs, surgery and physiotherapy; a move to a more healthy environment (the Victorians were very keen on that one); nutrition, and the revival of purpose and morale. But none of these is essentially divine healing, because healing that conforms to the biblical pattern results from the direct action of God, and not from human effort, science or common sense–however useful these may be in their own way. *Divine healing is a spiritual work*, achieved by the indwelling divine life that replaces the spirit of infirmity and decay. *It is God's healing.*

The roots of healing

Divine healing is one of the great fundamental teachings of the Bible. The first explicit reference to it comes in Genesis with the healing of King Abimelech, whose people had been struck with sterility after he took Abraham's wife. The last comes in the third letter of John where he writes to

Gaius: 'I would that ye be in health, even as thy soul prospereth' (3 Jn. 3). Between these two are found over six hundred and fifty references to sickness and health, in both the Old and New Testaments.

At the centre of the ministry of divine healing stands Jesus. The Gospels are crammed with stories relating how Jesus healed every sort of illness, and anyone who has read them will be able to see in his mind's eye the cripples picking up their beds and the blind dancing for joy. But Jesus wasn't just a kind of walking casualty clinic; the nature of the healings, and the fact that healing itself was not always a priority, show that they formed part of a larger plan, and this plan in turn sheds light on the meaning of healing.

A good place to start a study of the healing work of Jesus is Matthew 8. The first section comes at the end of the long teaching passage in Matthew called the Sermon on the Mount. Descending from the mountain Jesus is met by a leper who worships him and declares his belief that Jesus can, if he wishes, heal him of the disease. Clearly, we are given in this story an object lesson in faith, but there is more to it than that, because leprosy in Israel was symbolic of sin (remember Miriam and Gehazi), and so Christ's response 'I will; be thou clean' has a double edge to it, as also does his command that the man go to the priests, as the law dictated, 'for a testimony unto them'. The physical healing was a sign of a greater spiritual healing; in fact it was in a way a proof of it, since Jesus in another passage declares a sick man free of his sins before restoring him physically, to show that forgiveness was not just a matter of words.

Another light on this is provided by verse 17 where Matthew connects the healing ministry of Christ to a famous prophecy of Isaiah. The Messiah, it says, 'took our infirmities and bare our sicknesses.' The passage from which this is taken, Isaiah 53, again blends together physical and spiritual healing, for the Messiah is also pictured as 'wounded for our transgressions . . . bruised for our iniquities' (Isa. 53:5). Luke picks up the same thread in the summary statement, 'The Son of Man is not come to destroy men's lives, but to *save* them' (Luke 9:56 KJV). The greek word used here, *sozo*, means more than just to 'keep from damnation' in the narrow theological sense. It means to deliver, to preserve, to heal, give life, make whole. In other words, God's gift to mankind is not the simple ticket to heaven, but a total renewal, or making whole, of which present physical healing is a sign as well as an intrinsic part.

Christ's healing, therefore, was of a piece with his saving work, not a 'PR' job to make the gospel more interesting. Where there is salvation for our sons, there also is healing for our bodies. They are two sides of exactly the same coin. And just as salvation comes to us through no merit of our own but by the free action of divine grace, so healing comes by the word, power and mercy of God, who gives and can take away as he chooses. In verses 5 to 10, for instance, we see a Roman centurion asking Jesus to heal his servant. The man knew he had no rights over Jesus; he could not demand that he speak the healing word and expect to receive it. Like all of us he made his request with only one thing to recommend him: humble faith.

This is a vital word. The centurion was a military man accustomed to the notions of authority and obedience – if he wanted his boots cleaned he told someone to clean them and they got on with it; if he needed to get some groceries he told someone to buy them and they went. It was as simple as that. But he wasn't foolish enough to think his men obeyed him for any power or importance he possessed in himself. On the contrary his authority over them hung on the fact that others – higher officers, generals, and ultimately Caesar – had authority over *him*. He belonged to the hierarchy of the Empire. It was only natural, then, that he should see Jesus as a man under authority just as he was, the difference being that for Jesus the chain of command ended not with the Emperor, but with God. From this point of view it was no surprise (in fact it was almost logical) that when Jesus commanded healing with the full weight of divine authority behind him it should happen at the double.

Simplistic? Maybe, but he'd hit on the essential characteristic of faith: 'Verily, I say unto you, I have not found so great faith, no, not in Israel.'

It is virtually impossible to read the stories of Christ's ministry without seeing this link between faith and healing. 'Believe ye that I am able to do this?' he asks the two blind men (Matt. 9:28); and comforting Jairus, the ruler of the synagogue, whose daughter was already dead, he says, 'Fear not: believe only, and she shall be made whole' (Luke 8:50). The message is clear: willing faith invites healing, and hard-hearted scepticism such as he found in his own country of Nazareth obstructs it (Mark 6:5). And what he practised in his own ministry he fully expected his disciples to practise in theirs. His final instructions to them in Mark 16 are rendered in the New English Bible, 'Faith will bring with it these miracles . . . the sick on whom they lay their hands will recover.' That the disciples took it seriously is clear from their writings in the New Testament. James had no doubt that 'the prayer of faith shall save the sick,' (James 5:16), and Paul reckoned the shield of faith (Eph. 6:16) to be the Christian's strongest defence against the devil.

But there is one more lesson in Matthew 8. To be saved or physically healed isn't a private blessing to be stored away in some safe place, never to see the light of day; it is to be broadcast and publicised as a testimony of God's love and grace. The leper did it in going to the priests, and so, with different results, did the demoniac mentioned at the end of the chapter. This man had for years been an uncontrollable brute, so fierce that chains would not bind him and anyone passing by his makeshift home among the tombs did so at considerable risk. But that did not mean the locals were happy to see him healed. When Jesus set him free of his devils in the celebrated incident of the swine rushing hysterically into the sea, the people from the nearby city came out *en masse* to request that Jesus go away. This is in one way a reminder that our witness, even to something as wonderful as a healing, will not always be well received. From the sceptic's standpoint, to see a person suffering in what you suppose to be a cruel, Godless universe is sometimes more acceptable than to be obliged by his healing to admit there is a God who loves and cares, and who may be interested not just in others but in your personally.

Healing in Scripture

An early reference to healing in the Old Testament is in one of the names of God, given in Exodus 15 verse 26. It was revealed to the Israelites when, three days after the glorious victory over Egypt at the Red Sea, they arrived at Marah to find that the springs were bitter. A cry went up against Moses, presumably that they were about to die of thirst and feared that God had led them out of Egypt only to bring on them the same judgment he had brought on the Egyptians. Moses prayed, and was shown a tree whose timber would make the waters sweet. The incident became a lesson for the Israelites: 'If thou wilt diligently hearken to the voice of the Lord thy God, and wilt do that which is right in his sight, and wilt give ear to his commandments, and keep all his statutes, I will put none of these diseases upon thee, which I have brought upon the Egyptians: for I am the Lord that healeth thee.' The last phrase is the divine title; it might be translated 'I am *the Lord thy physician.*'

At Marah God wasn't simply playing on the Israelites' nerves to make them tow the line, for the specific promise linking careful obedience to bodily health is repeated twice elsewhere. First in Exodus: 'And ye shall serve the Lord your God, and he shall bless thy bread, and thy water; and I will take sickness away from the midst of thee' (Exod. 23:25). Then in the covenant book Deuteronomy: ' . . . If thou hearken to these judgments . . . the Lord will take away from thee all sickness and will put none of the evil disease of Egypt, which thou knowest, upon thee; but will lay them upon all them that hate thee' (Deut. 7:12, 15). The promises were actually fulfilled on more than one occasion – in the recovery of the repentant Miriam, and in the plague of fiery serpents recounted in Numbers 21. In the second case there is a strong element of faith since the healing of the victims was conditional upon their getting up and looking at the brass serpent Moses had made. Presumably some of the Israelites perished in spite of the offer of healing, because they simply didn't believe it.

The general health of the Israelites during the wilderness period is attested in Psalm 105 Verse 37: 'He brought them forth also with silver and gold: and there was not one feeble person among their tribes.' In the subsequent history of the nation healing came in the form of individual miracles. In the course of his stay with the widow in Zarephath, Elijah raised her son from the dead (1 Kings 17.22), and his successor, Elisha, did the same with the child of a Shunammite woman who had fallen on his head when out reaping with his father (2 Kings 4:34). Elisha also healed the Syrian general Naaman of leprosy using, as Moses had with the serpent, a simple action which was really a test of the man's faith (2 Kings 5). An interesting feature of this story is the role of Naaman's servants in encouraging him to bathe in the Jordan. Naaman's personal pride was such that he could hardly accept healing without some acknowledgement of his status; the prophet would have to make a great palaver about the healing, or send him off to accomplish some feat of valour. Anything was better than being ducked seven times in a stream tht wasn't even on the Syrian map. His servants were more practical. All right, they said, the Jordan may not be your private jacuzzi – but what have you got to lose?

A more elaborate healing occurred with King Hezekiah through Isaiah the son of Amoz (2 Kings 20). Here the distinguishing feature is the faith of the sick man himself, or more precisely his misery in the face of death. Isaiah at first showed him no particular sympathy: God had decided his time was up and rather than sit around moping he should get his affairs in order. But Hezekiah would have none of it. He protested and wept so much that Isaiah had barely reached the middle court of the palace before God sent him back to say he had been granted another fifteen years. Isaiah then instructed the servants to put a compress of figs on

Hezekiah's boil, as a result of which he recovered – much to the amazement of the messengers of Berodach-baladan, king of Babylon, who had been sent to Jerusalem with the Old Testament equivalent of flowers and a get-well card.

But if God was *Jehovah-rapha* to his people – the God who healed them – it was a breach of faith on their part to seek healing anywhere else. This explains why Elijah dealt out such rough justice to the servants of Ahaziah, the king who had fallen through the lattice of an upper chamber and wanted the god of Ekron to predict his chances of survival. When the prophet reached the royal sickbed he wasn't bringing chocolates: 'Forasmuch as thou hast sent messengers to enquire of Baal-zebub the god of Ekron, is it not because there is no God in Israel to enquire of his word? Therefore thou shalt not come down off that bed on which thou art gone up, but shalt surely die.' (2 Kings 1:16). A similar fate befell King Asa of Judah, though in this case the judgment was implicit; '. . . his disease was exceeding great: yet in his disease he sought not to the Lord, but to the physicians' (2 Chron. 16:12).

Israel's persistent disobedience to God's law was the formal cause of her people's sickness, and one reason why healing was viewed more and more by the prophets as a provision of God's future kingdom rather than the present one. Isaiah, for instance, says of that new Zion, 'The inhabitant shall not say, I am sick: the people that dwell therein shall be forgiven their iniquity' (Isa. 33:24). Not surprisingly Jesus used these prophecies to announce the start of his own ministry, the coming to earth of the new Kingdom of God. Quoting Isaiah 61 in the synagogue he says, 'The Spirit of the Lord is upon me, because he hath anointed me to preach the gospel to the poor; he hath sent me to heal the brokenhearted, to preach deliverance to the captives, and recovering of sight to the blind, to set at liberty them that are bruised . . . ' (Luke 4:18). Total restoration, in the power of the Spirit, made possible through the atonement. How important physical healing was in his ministry is indicated by the reply he gave to John the Baptist's disciples, who had come for reassurance that Jesus really was the Christ. 'Go your way, and tell John what things ye have seen and heard; how the blind see, the lame walk, the lepers are cleansed, the deaf hear, the dead are raised, to the poor the gospel is preached' (Luke 7:22). If healing of the body wasn't the centre post of his ministry it was nonetheless an essential support. As Harnack once said, 'Jesus appeared among his people as a physician.'

The scale of his healing was phenomenal. He dealt with a whole range of ailments from demon possession to physical injury, and mighty cures were effected. The methods he used varied with the occasion. Of the many men and women he encountered in the Gospels, eight he healed by touch, seven with a word, three with a simple ceremony involving spitting and touching the patient. Eleven times the sick were brought by their friends, six times they came by themselves; most were healed instantaneously, one by stages, one gradually. Healings were clear-cut restorations of physical infirmity. At no time did Jesus use scientific or medical means to impart healing – he simply presented himself as an object of faith and healed those who believed. One thing links together all of his healing acts, though – the special motive of love for lost and suffering human beings. As Matthew records, 'When he saw the multitudes, he was moved with compassion on them' (Matt. 9:36).

With a track record like that it is remarkable that he should have said to his disciples, 'He that believeth on me . . . greater works than these shall he do; because I go unto my father' (John 14:12). But during his earthly ministry he had prepared his followers for this work, sending them out on his third Galilean tour to 'heal the sick, cleanse the lepers, raise the dead, cast out devils' (Matt. 10:8). And it seems that in the days after the first Pentecost a great tide of healing swept through the church, for ' . . . by the hands of the apostles were many signs and wonders wrought among the people . . . insomuch that they brought forth the sick into the streets, and laid them on beds and couches that at least the shadow of Peter passing by might overshadow some of them. There came also a multitude . . . and they were healed every one' (Acts 5:12–17). On six further occasions in Acts Luke records these signs and wonders pouring out at the hands of the Christian community, leaving little doubt that at the close of the New Testament period healing was regarded as an important feature of evangelism by the men and women who, in obedience to the Lord's command, carried the gospel of salvation to the ends of the earth.

What happened to it after this we shall see a little later on.

Why divine healing?

Many of the purposes of divine healing have already been hinted at in the scriptures I have quoted. If we draw all these together they fall into five main categories.

(1) It is a natural expression of God's love that he should have compassion on his people and want to heal them. We read of Jesus that he 'was moved with compassion and healed all who were sick', and God moves through his servants today for exactly the same reason. He heals because he loves us with an everlasting love, and healing is part of his redeeming purpose for mankind.

(2) Healing is part of God's attack on Satan, from whom all sickness is ultimately derived. As John writes, ' . . . the Son of God was manifested, that he might destroy the works of the devil' (1 John. 3:8). The Church continues Christ's work in his name and in his strength.

(3) Miracles of healing provide a witness to the truth of the gospel. The writer of Hebrews refers to believers preaching the gospel, 'God also bearing them witness, both with signs and wonders, and with divers miracles, and gifts of the Holy Ghost . . . ' (Heb. 2:4), and Jesus himself urges his hearers, if they do not believe his claims, to 'believe the works: that he may know, and believe, that the Father is in me, and I in him' (John 10:38). The

gospel is not a matter of clever arguments, but of the power of God that changes lives.

(4) The ministry of healing is exercised within as well as around the church. Supporting the gospel, healing miracles add conviction to the word; but for those who already believe they are a comfort and an assistance. James makes this clear when he recommends that the sick Christian call for the elders of his church to anoint him with oil, because the prayer of faith saves the sick, 'and if he has committed sins, they shall be forgiven him' (James 5:15).

(5) Finally, healing acts as a beacon for the gospel, attracting attention to it. People flocked to Jesus not in the first instance because he was a great teacher, but because they had heard rumours of his miracles. The chance of seeing a miracle even aroused Herod's interest. The same thing happened with the early apostles; when Philip, driven from Jerusalem by the fury of persecution, landed in the city of Samaria, 'the people with one accord gave heed unto those things which Philip spake, hearing and seeing the miracles which he did' (Acts. 8:6).

Today nothing has changed. Healing still expresses God's love, comforting the believer, beating down the devil, announcing and substantiating the gospel. I have seen it work in all these ways myself, countless times, with countless people. No one is exempt. I have seen healing come to members of the House of Lords, to Royalty, television personalities, actors, doctors, lawyers, mayors, opera singers and pop stars; I have also seen it come to drug addicts, alcoholics, prostitutes, gays and criminals. Everyone from the highest to the lowest and all of the ordinary folk in between. Healing brings God's transforming power into the lives of human beings wherever it is unleashed. In fact Elsie Salmon, a renowned healing evangelist in South Africa thirty years ago, said that 'a spiritual revival could not come in a better way than through the healing of body, soul, mind and spirit. This is the greatest challenge the church has received in this generation.'

I could pick on a thousand stories to illustrate the range of the healing gift in its effect on the churches and communities I visit. The one I have chosen is short, simple and touching. When I visited Newcastle a while ago I spoke about the need for healing in families and broken homes, without knowing that there sat in the audience a woman who had left her husband and four year old daughter to live with another man in Tyneside. She came forward when I gave the appeal, and left her lover that very night. What neither of us knew was that at the same moment she stood at the altar, he husband, who was not a Christian, was on his knees 35 miles away praying with his little daughter. Apparently her very words were, 'Lord, make Mummy worry, and bring her home tomorrow.' They didn't know about the crusade, they hadn't even heard of me. But the next day the mother returned home and today they are a happy, *healed* family.

Healing comes in all forms, but it is always God answering our prayers.

4: Healing in History

The Lord has a long arm, and infinite love . . .

Isabel Chapman

In the first years following Christ's ascension his disciples believed he would return very soon. Their Master had after all said of the coming tribulation: 'This generation shall not pass, till all these things be fulfilled' (Matt. 24:34) and the persecutions they suffered under Roman emperors like Nero and Domitian must have made it seem that the crisis was upon them. 'These are the beginning of the sorrows. Then shall they deliver you up to be afflicted, and shall kill you: and ye shall be hated of all nations for my name's sake' (Matt. 24:8, 9). This produced in the Christian community a sense of urgency and excitement. Since they lived in a world order that was on the brink of collapse there was little to be said for settling in for a long stay. After a short flurry of evangelism and persecution God would blow the whistle and everything belonging to the imperfection of the old world – including the spiritual gifts – would be swallowed up in the new. 'For we know in part, and we prophesy in part,' wrote Paul to the Corinthians. 'But when that which is perfect is come, then that which is in part shall be done away' (1 Cor. 13:9, 10).

As time went on, though, the apostles died and the church found its persecutions separated by periods of relative peace and tolerance. Since Christ did not come back, his followers had to come to terms with living and working in a world they did not belong to but none the less still occupied. In many ways this was good for them;

in the next two or three centuries they got together and decided on a lot of important things – like exactly what they believed – and their decisions have since stood the church in good stead. But there were disadvantages as well. Exchanging the bivouac for something more like a permanent camp made life seem a bit humdrum and routine. True, they had to be ready every moment for Christ's return, but without the persecutions that kept them on the knife edge of expectancy and hope it was safer to assume he wasn't going to come just yet, and that some of their energy should go into the practical (but still godly) activities of working, worshipping and raising children. Gradually, and for reasons that have not been preserved to us, the use of spiritual gifts in the church faded – and with them the gift of miraculous healing.

But they have never been lost altogether. Fairly frequently over the last two thousand years an individual or a movement has come to the notice of the church through an unusual ability to bring physical healing. And enough of these cases have been recorded to give us at least a general picture of the healing ministry as it has been exercised between the apostolic period and our own. This chapter gives a brief résumé.

Up to the Middle Ages

The Church Fathers, the pastors and theologians who led the church until about the time Christianity was made the official religion of Rome, left considerable quantities of writing which suggests they took the ministry of healing for granted as a normal part of the Christian experience. Because the first of them, Justin Martyr, was born in the early second century, there is a slight gap in our knowledge between his writings and the last books of the New Testament, which were almost certainly completed before the end of the first. Justin makes it very clear, however, that the healing of demoniacs was not unusual in his day. He wrote in about 150AD:

> 'And now you can learn this from what is under your own observation. For numberless demoniacs throughout the whole world, and in your city, many of our Christian men exorcising them in the name of Jesus Christ, who was crucified under Pontius Pilate, having healed, and do heal, rendering helpless and driving possessing demons out of men, though they could not be cured by other exorcists and those who used incantations and drugs.'

A similar view is expresed by Irenaeus, Bishop of Lyons, who died in about 180 AD:

> 'Some do certainly and truly drive out devils, so that those who have been cleansed from evil spirits frequently both believe in Christ . . . and join themselves to the church . . . others still heal the sick by laying on of hands, and are made whole . . . the dead have even been raised up, and remained with us for many years.'

Because Christianity had by this time spread over most of the Roman world we find Christian writings in this period originating from places well away from Israel. In 200 AD, Clement, another philosopher, wrote from Alexandria in Egypt, and Tertullian from the ancient city of Carthage in North Africa. Both were familiar with the ministry of healing; for instance, Clement gave the following advice to Christians at prayer:

> 'Let them, therefore, with fasting and prayer, make their intercessions, and not with well-arranged and fitly ordered words of learning, but as men who have received the gift of healing, confidently to the glory of God.'

Tertullian had also come across deliverance:

> 'For the clerk of one of them, who was liable to be thrown upon the ground by an evil spirit, was set free from his affliction as was also the relative of another, and the

> little boy of a third. And how many people of rank, to say nothing of the common people, have been delivered from devils and healed of diseases?'

Of all the Early Church Fathers perhaps none was a more formidable theologian than Origen (183–253AD). But even his preoccupation with the doctrine of the church and standardising the text of the Old Testament did not prevent him from making this observation:

> 'Some Christians give evidence of their having received through faith a marvellous power by the cures which they perform. By this means we too have seen many persons freed from grievous calamaties, and from distraction of mind and madness and countless other ills, which would be cured neither by man nor demons.'

Finally we come to Augustine, probably the most famous of Christian teachers in this period. His conversion to the Christian faith from pagan philosophy was accomplished with the aid of his mother's enduring prayer, and deserves to be called a miracle in its own right. But although he turned whole heartedly to the gospel he did not immediately embrace the doctrine of divine healing. Only in later life did experience teach him otherwise: 'So we see there are miracles at this day wrought by God, with what means He likes best, who wrought them of yore.' Augustine seems to have witnessed a number of healings; he recounts the healing of a blind man in Milan and reports twenty others, adding that these are only a tenth of the stories he could relate.

But already at this period a change was taking place in the attitude Christians took to miracles of healing. Miracles came to be attributed to particular holy men, often hermits, who enjoyed the same reverent attention paid in previous ages to prophets and seers. To our modern eyes these men seem very peculiar, following a form of Christianity so severe that their nearest parallel today would be the Tibetan monk. One of them, called Daniel, was born in 409 AD; he entered a monastery at the age of twelve, and after spending twenty-five years there moved to Constantinople, the centre of the Eastern Church, where, inspired by the example of Simeon Stylites, he mounted a stone pillar on which he lived out the remaining three decades of his life. Rich and poor alike sought his counsel, and he is credited with many miracles of healing.

Another hermit, Theodore of Sykeon, who was born a century later in Galatia, practised an even more extreme asceticism, spending much of his time suspended from a rock in a narrow cage. This afforded him no shelter from the winter storms, and as if that were not punishment enough he often loaded himself with irons, undertook lengthy fasts, and observed a strict routine of psalm-singing. His efforts won him such respect from the local population that he became the leader of a monastic community and finally a bishop, though he gave up the second post after eleven years because the administrative duties got in the way of his prayer. Like Daniel he was much sought after, even by emperors, and accomplished many miracles.

The fact that we respond to accounts like these with astonishment and some scepticism indicates that they differ from those put forward by Augustine and the early Early Church Fathers. It's not just that the stories are bizarre; we sense that the miracles and the hermits who performed them were being looked at in a different way – almost as though the miracles were valued for their own sake and not as part of the gospel of salvation. And it is certainly true that as Europe slipped into the Dark Ages, although the ministry of healing as it is described in the New Testament became ever more rare, none the less popular interest in miracles of all kinds greatly increased. The decline in learning that took place during this era of political chaos and invasion, and the widespread misery of common men and women, probably combined to give this interest its distinctly superstitious flavour. The first signs were already around in Augustine's time. In 415 AD bones exhumed in Jerusalem were identified as those of Stephen, deacon and first martyr of the church, and in accordance with pagan practice were distributed throughout North Africa and Italy. Sooner or later miracles were claimed at each of the places to which the bones had been taken; and it wasn't long before the collection of holy relics had become a fad, and the lucrative trade in splinters from the real cross and saints' nail-parings started up in earnest. In the ensuing years a great many other superstitious methods of ensuring health and healing were adopted, among them the wearing of communion bread, or its consumption in large quantities as a sort of tonic. Baptismal water was drunk after use to promote health and vitality, and anointing oil blessed with ever longer and more elaborate rituals. In the later medieval period oil alone was considered insufficient to mediate the power of healing and was mixed with water and dust from the site of a past martyrdom.

Under the weight of this complex blend of faith and formula it is hardly surprising that the gift of healing nearly vanished from the church. But although it did not disappear entirely (St Bernard of Clairvaux (1090–1153), St Francis of Assisi (1191–1226), St Catherine of Sienna (1347–1380) and St Francis Xavier (1504–1552) are all known to have ministered or witnessed miracles of healing) it is significant that it sprang up more often than not in movements that rejected the hidebound formalism of the Roman church. One such group was founded by a man called Peter Waldo. A wealthy merchant and citizen of Lyons, Waldo went to a theologian rather as the rich young ruler of the Gospels had gone to Christ, and asked the way to heaven. He received the same answer: 'If thou wilt be perfect, go sell that thou hast, and give to the poor.' To his credit, Waldo took the command seriously. When he had paid off his creditors and made provision for his family he took to the streets to live in poverty as a beggar. In a short time a band of followers gathered around him, styling themselves the Waldensees, or 'Poor men of Lyons', and these he sent out preaching as Christ had sent the apostles, with no stave, purse or extra coat. The message they took had been gleaned by Waldo from his study of the New Testament. It was not the sort of thing that would endear them to the church authorities: they saw the Roman church as corrupt, wanted prayers in a language people could understand, thought nothing of allowing women to preach, and saw no reason to restrict the administration of communion to the priesthood. In short, this was a movement of renewal, and carried with it many features of renewal as we know it today – including the use of divine healing:

> 'Therefore concerning this anointing of the sick, we hold it as an article of Faith, and profess sincerely from the heart that sick persons, when they ask it . . . be joined by ones in prayer . . . that it may be efficacious to the healing of the body . . . and profitable.'

From the Reformation

The Waldensees ran into trouble first with the Bishop of Lyons, and later with the Pope himself. He approved of their vows of poverty but could not allow their preaching in the sees of hostile bishops, and when they disregarded this sanction he was left with little alternative but to excommunicate them. The old Roman church was still too powerful for dissenters to hold out against it. But Waldo, in his insistence on returning to Scripture as a source of authority, foreshadowed a much stronger movement which was to split the old church down the middle: the Protestant Reformation.

Its chief architect, Martin Luther, was critical of much of the superstitious practice of the medieval church, but he was in favour of the principle of divine healing. Healing to Luther was a literal, physical reality, appropriated on the spiritual level. 'How often it has happened,' he wrote, 'and still does, that devils have been driven out in the name of Christ; also by calling on his name and prayer, that the sick have been healed.'

Luther was followed by a string of Protestant Ministers

who discovered that divine healing happened not through dubious holy relics and incantations but as the New Testament said it did – by faithful prayer. Take, for example, this account of a miraculous healing from the journal of the Quaker evangelist George Fox:

> 'I went to a meeting at Arnside where (I found) Richard Myer, who had been long lame of one of his arms. I was moved of the Lord to say unto him amongst all the people, "Stand upon thy legs" (for he was sitting down): and he stood up, and stretched out his arm that had been lame a long time, and said "Be it known unto you, all people, that this day I am healed."'

Similarly Count Zinzendorf wrote at the turn of the seventeenth century:

> 'To believe against hope is the root of the gift of miracles; and I owe this testimony to our beloved church that apostolic powers are there manifested. We have had undeniable proofs thereof in the unequivocal discovery of things, persons and circumstances, which could not humanly have been discovered, in the healing of maladies in themselves incurable, such as cancers, consumptions, when the patient was in the agonies of death . . . all by means of prayer, or a single word.'

Divine healing came to characterise whole movements, as it had with the Waldensees. It is written of the Huguenots, the French Calvinist group that suffered dreadful persecution when the Edict of Nantes was revoked in 1685, that 'They who in their exile carried their mechanical arts and inventions into England, to the great blessing of the nation, carried here and there the lost art of supernatural healing, to the wonder of the Church of Christ.' The same was true of the early Moravians, who knew that spiritual gifts had not died out with the apostles:

'We are sure, that so far from being possible to prove by Scripture, or by experience, that visions and dreams, the gift of miracles, healings and extraordinary gifts have absolutely ceased in Christendom since apostolic times, it is on the contrary proved, both by facts, and by Scripture, that there be always these gifts where there is faith, and that they will never be entirely detached from it.'

It was a discovery that the preacher Hans Egede was to make in the next century. He arrived in Greenland in 1721 and was the first to preach the gospel to the Eskimos. To start with he had little to show for his efforts, until, attempting to prove to them the power of the gospel, he 'sought of God the gift of healing'; to his great satisfaction he soon saw scores of people healed, with the result that almost the entire population of Greenland was won over to Christ.

By that time, of course, the most famous revival of the eighteenth century was under way, led by John Wesley. Wesley's journal contains over two hundred descriptions of healings, some of them so spectacular that even he was amazed. On one occasion he records of a man with cancer that 'while they were praying for him he was at once healed of several tumours . . . . Our Lord never wrought a plainer miracle, even in the days of his flesh.' For his own ailments Wesley was in the habit of using anointing oil as prescribed by James (5:14, 15). 'This was another great means of continuing my health,' he wrote in his *Notes on the New Testament*, 'until I was about seven and twenty. I then began spitting blood, and continued for several years. Eleven years after, I was in the third stage of consumption; it pleased God in three months to remove this also. This God hath wrought.'

He also gives this striking account of his recovery from an attack of fever:

'I found myself much out of order; however, I made shift to preach in the evening; but on Saturday my strength failed, so that for hours I could hardly lift up my head. Sunday, the tenth, I was obliged to lie down part of the day, being easy only in one position. In the evening, besides the pain in my head and back and the fever which continued upon me; just as I began to pray, I was seized with such a cough that I could hardly speak; at the same time it came strongly into my mind, "These signs shall follow them that believe." I called on Jesus loudly to increase my faith, and confirm the Word of his grace. While I was speaking my pain vanished, the fever left me, my bodily strength returned, and for many weeks I felt neither weakness nor pain. Unto thee O Lord do I give thanks.'

The ministry of healing was stirred up again in the nineteenth century by the unorthodox Mother Ann, founder of the Shaker movement; by Pastor Johann Blumhardt, and by Dorothea Trudell. The last two set up homes of healing in Germany and Switzerland respectively. In fact, so complete and satisfactory were the cures effected at the Swiss homes of healing that Trudell was able to withstand a court action to have them declared illegal.

Since then the tradition of divine healing has been fairly continuous, and the list of Christian ministers and evangelists making use of it in the past and at the present time is too long to give in its entirety: men and women like Andrew Murray, Alexander Dowie, Smith Wigglesworth, Stephen and George Jeffreys, Douglas Scott, Percy Brewster, Fred Squires, Howell Harris, Arthur Williams, Aimmee Semple McPherson, Charles Price, Oral Roberts, Kathryn Kuhlman, Elsie Salmon, T. L. Osborne, Reinhard Bonnke, Morris Cerrullo, John Wimber and Dr Yonggi Cho, besides many others. Of course the fact that a man is used in the divine healing ministry does not mean that all his actions are defensible or every detail of his teaching flawless. People with the gift of healing have their faults and quirks like every other Christian. But there is no doubt that God has anointed them for their work, and their attitude to it is probably well summed up by William Booth, founder of the Salvation Army:

> 'There is not a word in the Bible which proves we may not have (gifts of healing and miracles) at the present time, and there is nothing in experience to show they would not be as usual today as in any previous period of Church history. No man, therefore, can be condemned for desiring them and the recent remarkable signs and wonders wrought amongst us not only demand, but shall have our most profound and sympathetic consideration. Far be it from me to say one word that would stay the longing of any heart for the extraordinary gifts already mentioned. I long for them myself; I believe in their necessity and believe they are already amongst us.'

How far they are accepted by the church at large is another question. Today most denominations have their healing orders, and some have ministers ordained and set aside for this particular work. But although the healing ministry has blossomed in the last thirty years it is still, when considered in the context of the whole task of the Christian church, relatively neglected. I have often said as a jibe that if the four men who lowered their paralysed companion down through the roof did so in many modern church services they would have to pull him out the same way. They'd probably be landed with a hefty repair bill too! Surely church leaders should pay attention when a renowned sceptic like Robert Ingersol says, 'Show me the signs and wonders and miracles of the Bible . . . and I will believe in Christianity.' They are the way forward for evangelism.

The rest of this book is devoted to understanding how these signs and wonders can be released.

5: The Healing Therapy

No one who is wise is ignorant of Bible teaching.

Samuel Chadwick

It is my conviction that healing begins with *words*.

As you can see by looking at this page or flicking on the television set there is no shortage of words in the modern world. There are probably far too many of them when you compare the torrent streaming from the presses with the time the ordinary man in the street has to take them in. In fact he very frequently reads a thousand words without 'taking them in' at all, because his brain is too small to accommodate everything he hears or reads, and it's simply too much bother to sort out the good stuff from the bad. How many of the trivial stories from the evening newspaper does the average commuter recall next morning? And if he hadn't been obliged to kill time in a crowded railway carriage would he have read half of them anyway?

There are though some words, or collections of words, that many people agree are worth reading. The word *free* for instance, marvellously concentrates the mind when featured prominently in an advertisement, and words like *sex*, *gay*, *vicar*, *horror*, *outrage*, *nude* and *scandal* (in almost any combination) can be placed at the head of a newspaper article with results favourable to the newspaper's publisher. If the publishers' notices are to be believed, as many as a million people at a time will read not just the same newspaper article, but a whole novel – perhaps four hundred pages of words – fast enough to put a completely different book on top of the bestsellers' list the following month. Writing of this sort is cherished by a faithful few and discarded as soon as read by everyone else. But occasionally a book sticks in our memories and becomes a 'classic' – not always because everyone has read it, but because everyone has heard of it and feels they ought to read it if they ever get the time. The late broadcaster Roy Plumley, who hosted the radio programme *Desert Island Discs*, allowed his castaways to take with them two works generally agreed to be the greatest classics in the English language – Shakespeare and the Bible. Shakespeare earned this distinction for being the only man to write a play composed entirely of memorable quotes; the Bible for fooling everyone that it's English literature when in fact it was written in Hebrew and Greek.

How central the Bible is to our British culture is demonstrated by the number of expressions it has given us which are used with equal facility by those who have read it and those who have not. The original 'feet of clay', for instance, belonged to the image in Nebuchadnezzar's dream (Dan. 2:31–45); when we pay 'lip service' to someone we are showing them the same insincere flattery the Pharisees showed to God (Matt. 15:8); and the first person to notice that ointment is spoiled by inquisitive flies was the writer of Ecclesiastes (10:1). Phrases like these have remained in common usage although at the present time the majority of English speaking people do not read the Bible regularly and would not regard it as particularly influential. And we only have to go back a few years to a time when ignorance of the Bible was the exception and not the rule. When Sir Walter Scott requested from his deathbed that his nephew read to him from 'the Book', the puzzled enquiry as to which book he meant was met with the firm rejoinder, 'There is only one Book!' Quite a concession from a famous author.

It is in fact remarked on quite often by men and women outside the church that the Bible has a depth and resonance no other work can match. This may have to do with the way its language pervades our everyday speech, but that is not the only explanation. The Bible is, after all, a book written under the inspiration of God, and if romantic novels appeal to our craving for love, and crime thrillers whet our appetite for mystery and adventure, it is hardly surprising that a book written to meet our deep-seated need of God shoud spark off in us a powerful and unexpected reaction. A good example of this is given by the actor Robert Powell, who played Christ in Zefferelli's film *Jesus of Nazareth*. Asked in an interview what it meant to him to play the part he replied: 'In portraying Christ I had to confront myself as never before with the question 'Do I believe?' I hadn't been to church since I was a child, and now I had to smother myself in the Bible. You can read the words in the Bible, but when you come to say them aloud, it is something else – they are *electric*.'

We should not conclude from this that there is a special magic about the words of the Bible, at least in any more than a metaphorical sense. The Bible explicitly condemns superstition, and that covers the Bible itself just as much as mirrors and salt: if you are ever unfortunate enough to be attacked by a vampire, repeating the Lord's Prayer won't help you any more than showing it a cross – both are superstitions! On the other hand, for those who by their faith are enabled to unlock the Bible's power and riches, its electric quality is very familiar. It is that sense of enormous relevance that comes – sometimes quite unexpectedly when words written hundreds of years ago in a completely different culture suddenly apply to our own personal situations here and now. It is God speaking in a score of voices – powerfully, softly, now with the strength of the whirlwind, now in the still small voice that calms and gives comfort.

Because God speaks through it in a special way the Bible must occupy a special place in the lives of Christian believers. It is like food: we grow strong by eating it, and when we lose our appetite for it we grow feeble and die inwardly. That is why the reading of the Bible and spiritual revival are so closely connected. In fact they are virtually inseparable. Once an Indian Christian travelling in the subcontinent tried to explain to his friends in another part of the country how the Lord was working in his home town. He meant to say they were having a revival, but by a fluke it came out as re*Bible*. The others immediately understood him, perhaps because he had hit on one of the essential ingredients of any spiritual awakening – that it is based on the example, preaching, teaching and obeying of Scripture.

Of course it works the other way around. When we ignore or discredit the Bible, our lives as individuals, the life of our church, and ultimately the life of our nation will suffer. We become lazy and spiritually impotent; we withdraw from our involvement in the church, leaving fewer and fewer men to bear the burdens of leadership. We add to the exodus from the churches and so help to undermine public confidence in Christianity as a source of moral values. We become victims of relativism, the belief that one man's moral code is as good as another's, and our society splits up into its various interest groups who, unrestrained by any absolute concept of right and wrong, resort to ever more brutal means to achieve their own ends. Truth, honesty and integrity are redefined to fit the individual's point of view. Crime and terrorism increase. And governments, no longer able to rely on prevailing Christian values to uphold law and order, are obliged to use force instead.

I'm not saying, of course, that the moment you stop reading your Bible you will turn into an uncontrollable hooligan. But the general trend to give less credence to God's word in Scripture inevitably makes room for some other basic value, and since this is very often self-interest, the behaviour of the population in general is likely to degenerate. The Duke of Edinburgh made this precise point twenty years ago: 'We had a greater unity in this country when we believed in the Bible, and in the days of God; but take away God and we return to tribalism again.'

It is a comment not without weight, especially in view of the miners' strike of 1984/5. What speaks most loudly in picket line violence is not the case being put forward by the pickets or the police but the methods they are willing to use to back it up, and the insistence in every confrontation that it was the man on the other side of the barricade who made the first aggressive move. Of course there were many issues at stake in this long and miserable affair and it is not my intention to exploit it as a simple example of man's inhumanity to man. None the less it is interesting to note that the counties experiencing the worst violence were also the ones where rates of church attendance are lowest. And since there is an intrinsic connection between church attendance and the degree to which God, through the Bible, is permitted to speak into the local community, it does indicate that a falling away from the word of God affects more than the size of the Sunday collection.

The word is the key

I said that healing begins with words, by which I mean God's word spoken through the words of the Bible. This is more than an observation that biblical faith promotes health and well-being in Christian, church and community, while the abandonment of Scripture prevents it. The relationship between the word of God and healing is specific and taught clearly in the Bible. 'My soul cleaveth unto the dust,' cries the psalmist, 'quicken thou me according to thy word' (Ps. 119:107). And in Proverbs: 'Whosoever despiseth the word shall be destroyed: but he that feareth the commandment shall be rewarded' (Prov. 13:13). Psalm 107 makes the connection plain: 'He sent his word, and healed them' (v. 20).

I believed there are times when this is literally true. There was a man dying in hospital from multiple haemorrhages who happened to see on his bedside locker a copy of the Gideons' Bible. He was too weak to pick it up, but he remembered from his childhood stories of Jesus healing the sick, so he reached out painfully until his hands lay on the cover, and whispered inwardly 'God of the Bible, if you are the same today . . . heal me . . . ' Only an hour later his bleeding had ceased; the doctors were able to give him blood transfusions, and within a few days he was back on his feet and able to leave hospital. He had put his trust in God through the word. It wasn't a magic Bible; it was just paper and card like any other book. But it contained God's words and his message of healing and salvation, and it became the means of that man's recovery.

Quite often in the services I take I sense that the congregation is not sufficiently aware of the promises and power of God as they are contained in the Scripture, and before laying hands on anyone I take my Bible down the healing line and ask people, whether they are sitting or standing, to place their hands on it and repeat after me that they believe it to be God's healing word – the word spoken by God himself in which they are putting their wholehearted faith. Not the book, but the promises God has spoken through it. His *word*.

But like many things in the Christian faith what is in one way supremely simple is in another way richly complex, and because this is so with God's word we should before we go any further explore some of these complexities.

First of all, God's word is *creative*. That is, it does more than communicate information in the way our words do: it actually moves out and accomplishes. Thus God stands at the centre of his creation rather as a managing director stands at the centre of his business empire. He speaks, and the whole structure responds to obey what is said. If the director says in his boardroom 'Go and buy a fleet of trucks,' someone leaps up to carry out his instruction. And when God said 'Let there be light' the primeval matter of which the universe was made suddenly shifted into a new form '. . . and there was light' (Gen. 1:3). So, as the psalmist says, 'By the word of the Lord were the heavens made; and all the host of them by the breath of his mouth' (Ps. 33:7). Every one of the new things we see flashing into existence in the first chapter of Genesis did so simply because God *said* it. 'He spake, and it was done; he commanded, and it stood fast.' (Ps. 33:9).

We know that much of the good work God did on these first six days of creation was undone in the fall – that what God spoke was then 'unspoken' by his disobedient creature, man. But the creative function of God's word did not cease with the sculpting of the universe, because Ezekiel makes it abundantly clear that it is God's word that will go out and recreate what man's sin has caused to wither and waste away.

In the midst of the valley of dry bones the prophet is told: 'Prophesy upon these bones, and say unto them, O ye dry bones, hear the word of the Lord. Thus saith the Lord God unto these bones; Behold, I will cause breath to enter into you, and you shall live . . . ' (Ezek. 37:4, 5).

Nor is the word of God restricted to creation. It is in a general way his agent, ready to do whatever he pleases in the context of his overall plan for the redemption of his world. Sometimes, as in the case of the plagues in Egypt, his purpose has been to correct and punish: one psalm recounts that in delivering his people from slavery to the Egyptians God 'spake, and there came divers sorts of flies, and lice in all their coats . . . He spake, and the locusts came, and caterpillars, and that without number . . . ' (Ps. 105:31, 34). On other occasions his word is sent out to achieve restoration and healing. The writer of Psalm 107 was probably referring to Israel's wanderings in the desert when he wrote, 'Fools because of their transgression and because of their iniquities are afflicted. Their soul abhorreth all manner of meat; and they draw near unto the gates of death.' But it is the word of the Lord that brings their healing: 'Then they cry to the Lord in their trouble . . . he sent his word, and healed them, and delivered them from their destructions' (Ps. 107:17–20).

So God's word goes out to do his work, to create, to re-create, to break down and to restore. It is the executive who can be relied upon to do exactly what the managing director requires. Says the prophet Isaiah: ' . . . as the rain cometh down, and the snow from heaven, and returneth not thither, but watereth the earth, and maketh it bring forth and bud, that it may give seed to the sower, and bread to the eater: so shall my word be that goeth forth out of my mouth: it shall not return unto me void, but it shall accomplish that which I please, and it shall prosper in the thing whereto I sent it' (Isa. 55:10, 11).

This image of the word is developed two ways in Scripture. On the one hand it comes to be seen as a written, and therefore a permanent and *changeless* word. This is because the words which God spoke through his servant Moses – the Law and the

Ten Commandments which make up a large part of Leviticus and Deuteronomy – were written down to form the 'constitution' of his people Israel. They were changeless words from the changeless God, and carrying a changeless promise of blessing for those who obeyed them. That is why the psalmist says, 'Thy word is a lamp unto my feet, and a light unto my path' (Ps. 119:105) and makes it a matter of firm religious practice that he should keep it: 'I will delight myself in thy statutes: I will not forget thy word' (v. 16). In the same tradition Jesus, being tempted by the devil to turn stones into bread, declared, 'It is written, man shall not live by bread alone, but by every word that proceedeth out of the mouth of God' (Matt. 4:4) – a statement that is doubly significant because the written word is seen by Jesus both as giving life and as providing a source of absolute authority.

For Christians, of course, the written word of God includes not only the Law but the entire Old Testament and the New Testament as well – the whole package wrapped up and labelled as *inspired*, or literally, *God-breathed*. This is part of the reason why the Bible is held in such high esteem in the Christian church, and acts as a special channel of spiritual power as it did for the man with the haemorrhages I mentioned earlier. But that is not the end of the matter; the image of the word is developed in a second and more important way, because 'God, who at sundry times and in divers manners spake in time past unto the fathers . . . has in these last days spoken unto us by his Son' (Heb. 1:1, 2). This final and most emphatic of God's statements to his world is none other than Christ himself, distinguished from all previous divine words by a capital letter: 'the Word was made flesh' (John 1:14).

In the New Testament, 'Word' is the translation of the Greek *Logos*. People of that period would have been very familiar with the term; besides being the ordinary Greek word for 'word' it was used by a group called the Stoics to describe a primitive power, or fiery vapour, which they imagined to inhabit and influence the universe and everything in it, rather as Christians believe the human spirit occupies the body. This was the nearest thing to a god in their scheme of things, an idea that must have been similar to the Force in *Star Wars*–though no Stoic would have gone about saying, 'The *logos* be with you!'

John gave the word an entirely new meaning. For him the *Logos* was no impersonal divine force, but a person who had existed from eternity with God the Father and who shared his godhead; whose sending to earth as the man we call Jesus was the most complete and powerful expression of his love that God could possibly have made. Long before God's word spoke the world into existence his Word, his *Logos*, was ready to redeem it. In fact it was the Word who said in the beginning 'Let there be light', for all God's creative speaking to man is rooted in that greatest of statements about himself, his Son Jesus Christ, the *Logos*. 'In the beginning was the Word, and the Word was with God, and the Word was God . . . All things were made by him; and without him was not anything made that was made' (John 1:1, 3).

This requires a little thought. It turns out that the executive, who obeys his managing director by going out and buying the fleet of trucks, is none other than the managing director himself. Perhaps it happens like this: after saying in the boardroom that he will buy the trucks the director makes an order by telephone, confirms the deal in a letter dictated to his secretary, and arranges a date to see the trucks delivered. So far the man at the truck company has had no personal contact with the directors at all; but when the trucks are ready the director goes down and receives them in person. Seeing him for the first time the man at the truck company says to himself, 'Aha, so this is the man who built that huge business empire. Before today I'd only spoken to him on the phone and read his letter, but now here he is in the flesh . . . '

This is really a rather poor analogy, but it does help us to see what John is saying. The *Logos* is God's executive, or God acting in the capacity of executive, to create the universe and finally to come in person as Jesus Christ to redeem mankind. All things were made by him, and in him all things will be redeemed. But there is more to it than that, because besides building the empire and coming to collect the trucks, the managing director wrote letters to tell his supplier what was going on; and in the same way mankind has been kept informed of God's activity down the ages by means of his inspired word, given through prophets and finally written down in the permanent record we now call the Bible. Jesus fulfilled the word of the Old Testament much as the director fulfilled his appointment by turning up to see the truck salesman; and today we can learn of God's work in Christ by reading Scripture just as the salesman could at a later date remind himself of the deal by going back over the correspondence.

That is why we Christians see double when we talk about God's word. There are really two kinds – God's spoken word (the Bible) and God's acted word (the *Logos*). The difference between them is vital, and complex enough to keep us thinking for a very long time. A brief summary comes out rather like a riddle: the Word inspired the word and fills the word, so to find the Word we should read the word and preach the word.

And healing, as John tells us, is something the Word attaches great importance to.

The healing word

There is no doubt at all that healing, being inherent in God's desire to redeem his people, is one of the most prominent features of Christ's ministry on earth. In fact if you edited out all the references to healing in the Gospels the result would be almost unintelligible. They record forty-seven individual healings, and seventeen occasions when Jesus is seen healing the multitude in what today would be called a mass healing service. 'Jesus went about all Galilee,' says Matthew, ' . . . healing all manner of sickness and all manner of disease among the people' (Matt. 4:23).

We have seen already that the ministry was continued by the apostles after Christ's ascension. How essential this was to the work of evangelism is demonstrated by the fact that of all Christ's commands to spread the gospel not a single one fails to mention healing as a following sign. 'In my name . . . they shall lay hands on the sick,' says Mark, quoting the words of Jesus; and then adds of the early Christian believers: 'they went forth, and preached everywhere, the Lord working with them and confirming the word' (Mark 16:17–18, 20). Nothing in Scripture indicates that this state of affairs was meant to change. Jesus Christ, the Word, is, according to the writer of Hebrews, 'the same yesterday, and today, and forever' (Heb. 13:8). The effects of the atonement, the resurrection and Pentecost have not weakened with the intervening years. What Paul wrote about the gifts of the Holy Spirit to the Corinthian church we can confidently expect to be true today, and every day until the close of the age, when this world is swept away in the founding of the new.

Why then are the spiritual gifts and the ministry of healing not in evidence in many churches today?

A lot of answers spring to mind: worldliness, the love of material things, discord, selfishness and loss of vision. But I believe one of the main causes of decline is what I have already alluded to in this chapter – the neglect of biblical teaching. Pastors often fail to preach the word of God from the pulpit, and congregations often fail to read it as part of their own devotions. Worse than that, scriptural instruction is sometimes discarded completely in favour of a more popular Christianity that concentrates on social and political issues instead of spiritual. Either course is fatal. Jesus was not using pretty figures of speech when he described himself as the bread of life and the living water. His rejoinder to the devil that a man lives by the words coming from the mouth of God meant precisely that God's word is nourishment to the soul; there is no excuse for calorie counting, and he did not expect his church to suffer from spiritual anorexia. A congregation draws its strength from the teaching it receives. 'A weak pulpit,' said Martin Lloyd-Jones, 'is a weak church'; and the Early Church Father St Jerome understood the relationship between word and Word very well when he said, 'Ignorance of Scripture means ignorance of Christ.' Ignorance of both together will starve off the spiritual gifts as surely as a drought turns your lawn brown.

Conversely the secret of a healthy church is a proper regard for the word of God. People who make much of the Scripture, who make it their food and drink and are fortunate enough to be taught soundly, will in the course of time enter into the fulness of New Testament experience – including the spiritual gifts of miracles and healing. The Bible is a well from which we are able to draw the waters of life. Like a well it may look relatively insignificant at the surface, but like the well its waters are constantly replenished so that no matter how much we use there is always more to spare. And it is to those who seek its refreshment, who with the psalmist say, 'Let not your word depart from our lips,' that God is able to give his transforming power.

It was in the old Christian magazine *Telescope* that I first came across that phrase. I remember the line clearly: 'The Bible was written for our transformation.' It's absolutely true – often startlingly so. Once, preaching through an interpreter in Marseilles, I heard a woman shouting in the crowd. She was saying, the interpreter told me, 'I can see, I can see!' I hadn't laid hands on anybody at that stage; I had simply been preaching the word of God, and the power of the Holy Spirit had come upon the woman and restored her sight – with six hundred witnesses to prove it. Here is one of the mysterious and wonderful things about the word of God in healing. Miracles don't happen because a healer touches a sick person, as if the touching completed a sort of electric circuit; nor is there a nebulous spiritual power which some gifted individuals can grasp and give out like lumps of plasticine. All these material images are inadequate. But the word of God contains – we might say, is pregnant with – the Word, the *Logos*, God's creative, executive power. And so when that word is preached in the Spirit of Christ it is quite likely that the Word with all his healing power will be released among those present – healing, breaking spiritual bondage, opening blind eyes, destroying sickness and deformity, delivering, revitalising, energising.

By the same token I believe that congregations who dwell in this atmosphere of worship in which the word is faithfully preached will be preserved from many of the illnesses that afflict others – though this is hard to demonstrate in practice, first because a careful scientific study would be needed to prove it, and second because for most church congregations this pitch of faithful, long term worship is still an ideal and not a living reality. A pastor I know said to me recently, 'I have taken my people through Revelation chapters 1 to 22, but they are still living outside of Revelation.' Perhaps a concerted effort to read and re-read the healing stories in the Gospels and Acts, and to live in them, would bear surprising results.

There is probably no better way to round off this study of the word of God in healing than to give a real-life example. This one is an extract from a letter sent to me by a Jewish family – whose background prepared them in a very special way for an encounter with the Word, and who found in it their healing and salvation:

> 'We are a Jewish Orthodox family. My wife Shirley was a very religious person. She loved all the traditions, laws and customs. She went to Israel at the age of twenty and worked in a kibbutz for six months. But she found the love of God was not foremost; many had other motives, many had problems they could not solve, and the threat of war was always hanging over us. Finally she came home due to constant illness. Since then she has raised much money and sent it to Israel.
>
> Eventually we met and were married. Later my wife contracted agrophobia and suffered greatly for some

years. She could not go out of the house on her own. We supported our religion, and I went regularly to the synagogue, my wife's father being a rabbi. Being strictly orthodox we did not mix with any other religious groups. My wife, however, was very ill; then through reading a Christian magazine she found Jesus Christ as her Saviour and Messiah.

Some months afterwards she asked me to take her to a large tent crusade led by Reverend Melvin Banks in Macclesfield. I asked friends what I should do. Some said 'Stay well away'. Others urged me to 'Give it a try.' I am a solicitor, well known in the community as a Jew, and well respected in the synagogue–so I do not want anyone to see me in a Christian meeting. I was comforted it was a marquee–I felt that among the hundreds of folk I would not be recognised! So I took my wife along, with my foster daughter Lynn who was mentally retarded.

I entered the great marquee and felt very much at home. Someone pointed out the Reverend Banks–he seemed a very ordinary fellow, dressed like ordinary people. He was chatting with folk, shaking hands and smiling. Finally came the service. I began to relax and be at ease as the people really sang and worshipped in a way I had never seen or felt before.

The effect of the preaching of the Bible upon me was indescribable. It had an inner conviction and compulsion upon me, both in revealing to me my deep inadequacy and sinfulness, and in developing confidence and immediate faith to receive God's pardon. All our lives were transformed that night!

The Lord saved us all. We have followed Jesus Christ from that day, and testify and stand for Christ everywhere we go. We have joined a Christian church, and since then my wife has had a wonderful healing, and my foster daughter was also completely healed from that night, with no mental troubles. In fact she has even grown physically–a retarded child who received a miracle from God and is well today. A wonderful miracle! We rejoice in Christ, the Messiah not only of the Jews but of the whole world!'

6: Power Through Your Faith

While you are doubting, you are not trusting; while you are trusting, you are not doubting.

Eric Dando

I want to begin this chapter about faith by telling you a little story. I didn't make it up; it is a true story, and in fact a very old one, because we know about it from a sheet of papyrus that remained hidden for many centuries in the caves of the Egyptian desert.

There was once a widow who lived in a house in the Nile valley. She was not especially rich, and so it was with great interest that she learned one day of some land being passed down to her. It was a large tract of land, and very fertile, but the trouble was she had no documents to prove her ownership. Consequently there seemed to be a large number of people around who believed it belonged to them and not to her. There was only one thing for it – to apply to a local magistrate and obtain a clear ruling on her rights. But this was not enough to stop them. The other claimants continued to make loud and persuasive pleas, so much so that she came to wonder if the land was really hers after all. In the end she decided to settle the matter by taking it to a higher authority – an Egyptian prefect. He ruled in her favour; and the letter he sent to tell her so still exists on a small scrap of papyrus. If anyone argued about the ownership from now on she had only to wave this document under his nose and that was that. She could prove her right to possession because she had written evidence to support it.

We may presume that she lived happily ever after. But what has that got to do with faith? Men and women of God have come up with some very servicable definitions of faith that don't need a story to make them clear. For Francis Dixon, for instance, faith is 'receiving all that Jesus has for us.' For Smith Wigglesworth, 'the word of God in action in our lives.' According to Charles Price it is a matter of 'standing actively on the promises of God', to Richard Baxter 'taking Christ at his word', and in the opinion of Martin Luther, who has as good a claim as any of them to be an authority on these things, faith is 'holding Christ and having him present in the here and now.' Why all this stuff about Egyptian prefects?

Go back to the writer of Hebrews. His very famous definition of faith runs like this: 'Faith is the substance of things hoped for' (Heb. 11:1). Actually the word he uses here for 'substance' is *hupostasis*, appearing only once in the Bible, and meaning, literally, 'that which stands under – and underpinning, a support, or applied figuratively as it is here, a guarantee or assurance. It is the same word that is used on the papyrus to describe the letter the widow received assuring her of full legal rights to her land. In that context it means 'title deed', or something very close to it, and by using this element in its meaning we may re-define faith as the *title deed* of things hoped for. Remember the widow had never seen the land she laid claim to. All she had to prove it belonged to her and not to anyone else was the letter from the prefect that said it was hers. And what do we have to prove that the promised salvation, the resurrection from the dead and the glory in heaven are really ours? After all, we can't see salvation; we can't prove by algebra that we will rise from the dead; we aren't yet treading the plains of heaven. So what have we got?

Answer: faith – the title deeds.

Faith needs to be distinguished sharply from nervous optimism. The two are very often confused. The man who arrives at a first night performance in the hope of getting a cancelled seat is nervously optimistic; the man who arrives with his ticket has faith. Of course there is a remote chance that the first man will finally get in, but while the other is lingering over his steak and kidney pie in a nearby restaurant he will be standing in a queue beneath his leaky umbrella, chewing his fingernails. One of the big benefits of faith is what it does to your state of mind. Which is why the physicist Albert Einstein, whose theory of relativity showed the world to be a good deal less predictable than Isaac Newton had imagined it, could say with equanimity, 'Our belief in Scripture is the firm basis upon which is founded our happy anticipation of good things to come.'

But since faith is commonly misunderstood, especially in connection with healing, we perhaps need to say a bit more about it. Having faith for healing isn't quite as simple as believing something is going to happen, as if by concentrating hard enough we could turn our hair green. The world is full of disappointed people who believed with all their heart that something was going to happen to them and didn't. So here are some important points to take in about faith.

Five lessons in faith

First, *faith is within*. As human beings we are able to do a great many different things. Our bodies enable us to perform every kind of physical action from pole vaulting to assembling watches; our minds give us the power of rational thought – that is, the ability to sort out a problem just by thinking about it; and our emotions allow us to respond to our situation with sorrow, anger or joy. All of these faculties are vitally important and we use them every day, particularly in our relationships with one another. But they are not the faculties we use in relating to God. We cannot touch God; we cannot learn much about him by exercising our minds; and although we may feel very strong emotions when we worship him it is not in the way we feel that our relationship with God consists.

We relate to God in that inaccessible place we often describe as our spirit and which men in biblical times called the heart. The Israelites were fairly clear as to where in the body their various faculties were placed; for example, they tended to locate feelings and emotions somewhere in the gut, or the 'bowels'. But the deepest, innermost part of a man, his essential being, they generally ascribed to his heart. That was where the roots of his character and his spark of life were to be found. Thus Jesus said, 'Out of the abundance of the heart the mouth speaks' and in response to the Pharisees' hypocrisy: 'This people honoureth me with their lips, but their heart is far from me' (Matt. 12:34; 15:8).

God has never wanted an obedience from man that deals in externals – saying the right prayers, making the right sacrifices, going to the right church. Obedience has to go all the way down to the bottom of the human personality. And in turning us to Christ he does not begin by changing what we think or what we feel (we can become Christians and for various reasons still be confused and unhappy); he begins with the heart. In Paul's words, he has 'sealed us, and given us the earnest of the Spirit in our hearts' (2 Cor.1:22). He treats the disease and not the symptoms, so that in the long run the symptoms will disappear for good.

But we should pay attention here. The 'earnest of the Spirit' will not be given to us willy-nilly, whether we like it or not. All the power of the Word of God, as it comes to us in Scripture for our healing and salvation, must be desired before it can be made effective. And here we come across a vital link in the healing chain – that of faith. Faith is a faculty neither of the body nor of the mind or emotions. It may cause us to feel certain things – relief or joy for instance – but it is not in itself an emotion. Nor is it a certain attitude of mind, although in nearly every case there is a point at which faith is recognised consciously and the man or woman who has it says suddenly, 'Yes, Lord Jesus, I accept your gift, I put my trust in you; save me and heal me.' Faith itself belongs to the heart. When we are first converted it usually takes the form of a deep inner conviction and certainty, a re-orientation of our whole being that happens sometimes outside our conscious control. C. S. Lewis had exactly this experience when he took a bus up Headington Hill in Oxford and realised when he got off at the top that he had become a Christian, almost in spite of himself.

Faith then is not something you can feel yourself into, or think yourself into. It is rooted in your innermost spirit and is an inward conviction of the heart. And so, with healing, for which it is every bit as important as it is for salvation, faith is not a technique for making yourself believe something is going to happen, but a total and deep-seated surrender to God in the trust that his will is for your healing and restoration.

Second, *we must use our potential for faith.* You may be saying at this stage, 'Well, that's all very nice, but I still don't think I have any faith, so maybe I should admit I'm not the sort of person to get it, and give up now.' The answer to this is that every man, woman and child on the face of this earth, whatever their age or condition, has the potential for faith. In fact we use faith constantly without even thinking about it. Did it occur to you, for instance, that that chair you're sitting on might have collapsed under you when you sat on it? Probably not, because your experience of chairs in the past led you to believe that provided it looked reasonably sturdy it would hold you up. In a very simple way you put faith in the chair, and not only in the chair, but also to some extent in its manufacturer and the goodwill of the person who owns it.

A better example is our faith in other people. Most of us regularly put our faith in a doctor by consuming whatever drug he prescribes for us, not usually pausing to wonder if he had his reading glasses on when he consulted the pharmaceutical directory, or whether he has an interest in bumping us off. We trust him as a person on the basis of what he has done in the past and whatever characteristics brand him in our opinion as a reliable chap. Anyway, the discomfort of the illness is usually more pressing than the possibility he might be poisoning us. (In all fairness I must add that when I used this illustration at a meeting in the East End of London, a

Cockney woman in the front row yelled out: 'He did poison me – that's why I'm here!' It took some time to get the audience quiet again.)

If we refused to use faith in our dealings with others life would quickly become impossible. There are no guarantees that a doctor will give you the right treatment, that a businessman will honour an agreement, or that your wife or husband really is working overtime and not in somebody else's bed. But if we didn't trust them we would live in a state of chronic anxiety, and become completely antisocial. Who would want to live with someone who constantly suspected them of infidelity? The result is that we are forced to trust, and in fact trusting does us good because it fosters friendship and builds up community.

There is no qualitative difference between that sort of faith and the sort we are asked to put in God. It's not even that we are asked to put a larger amount of faith in God – as Jesus said, you need faith no bigger than a grain of mustard to accomplish impossible things. What matters is steadfastness and consistency. Not wavering. Faith in God should not be shaken by anything we see or hear or feel; on the contrary it should in the long run be the motivating force behind all our thought and action. It should become a sort of fuel which by its continual outreach to God is continually replenished.

Third, *faith must be fed and renewed.* We sometimes forget that many of the things we do had originally to be learned. Today the art of reading will be so natural to you that you are unable to look at a page of print without understanding it; but when you were a small child, print – a page like this one you are reading now – would have been as incomprehensible to you as Egyptian hieroglyphics. What has brought you this amazing ability to extract from little black marks on a piece of paper words that you can pronounce and understand? Teaching and practice, of course. It's the same with everything. It's how you learn to drive a car, how you learn to talk, even to walk and eat.

Similarly, faith does not come to us naturally, even though life presents us with numerous opportunities to try it out. It may be a potential, but it is a potential that needs to be developed. Picasso's skill as an artist would never have seen the light of day had he not been able to cultivate it by learning the right methods and drilling himself with exercises so that the forms he drew on the canvas were just what he saw in his mind. And although we can't go to a spiritual art school there are three ways we can nourish our faith.

We can *feed it with the word of God.* 'If ye abide in me, and my words abide in you,' said Jesus to his disciples, 'ye shall ask what ye will, and it shall be done unto you' (John 15:7). The Bible is spiritual food. It builds us up, strengthens and encourages us. It also gives us greater understanding of the faith, greater maturity and wisdom. We will learn much not only by the regular reading, digesting and absorbing of Scripture, but also by studying good commentaries and listening to sound teaching. As Paul said, 'Faith cometh by hearing, and hearing by the word of God' (Rom. 10:17). Christians down the ages have attested the truth of this. John Wesley took the lesson so much to heart that he commanded his preachers, 'Preach faith until they get it!' And I myself can testify that regular reading of the Bible is of the most enormous benefit; I treasure God's word, and read it first thing every day – even before the morning paper!

Teaching, of course, needs to be put into practice, and that is why another way of developing faith is to *try it out*. You can read all about body building and eat all sorts of protein-rich food, but unless you get out there on the gym floor and start lifting the weights your biceps won't expand a single inch. And when James said to the early Christians, 'Faith, if it hath not works, is dead' (Jam. 2:17) he might as well have been talking about unworked faith as faith unsupported by good deeds. Faith thrives on activity and use, and withers through neglect. Mind you, the best way to start flexing the muscles of faith may not be to throw mountains into the sea. If we begin by believing God for smaller things, it will build up our confidence to trust him in greater things. And don't be discouraged by failure; no sportsman worth his salt gives up at the first defeat. Pick yourself up, learn from your mistakes, and try again.

Lastly, *strengthen faith by progress* in completely different virtues. This is a great encouragement, because we discover that faith is a gift of God as much as it is something to be found within ourselves. Alongside the love, joy and peace that grow in us as we walk in the Spirit there comes also faith (Gal. 5:22) – not a work, but a fruit; growing by a process we do not directly control, but still ours to enjoy.

Fourth, *faith will be positive.* You may not have heard about the pinball theory of human existence, which shows how things never work out the way we expect them to. It goes like this: you get shot out into the world, and are just beginning a graceful descent when – BAP! – something (let's say school) hits you and you fly off in another direction. You adjust your senses to all this new stimulation, then just as you're getting used to it – BAP! – and off you go somewhere else: adolescence. So it goes on in a long succession of formative experiences. You get your first heartbreak at thirteen – BAP! – failed O-levels at sixteen – BAP! – unemployment – BAP! – unhappy marriage – BAP! – mid-life crisis – BAP! – ulcers – BAP! – cancer – BAP! – GAME OVER – and nothing much to show for it. Your live is lived in a state of reaction, responding to things that happen to you, some of which you like and others you decidedly don't. The result is your personality develops calluses, peculiarities of character and behaviour, such as bitterness, fear and depression, which though common and familiar are predominantly negative.

The Christian is not at the mercy of circumstance, he is under the mercy of God – and that is a very different thing. Take the example of Peter, who seeing Jesus walking on the water wanted to get out of the boat and do the same. He wasn't acting impulsively; Jesus gave him express permission to do it. And as long as he thought about Jesus and trusted him, he stayed afloat. 'But when he saw the wind boisterous, he was afraid,' says Matthew (14:30). This was the crucial moment. Peter started to behave in reaction to the storm, and his feet sank along with his faith. So when Jesus caught hold of him, he didn't tick him off for taking unnecessary risks. He only said: 'O thou of little faith, wherefore didst thou doubt?' It was faith, positive in spite of the circumstances, and positive enough to overcome the circumstances, that would have kept Peter's feet dry. Doubt almost drowned him.

Fifth, *faith must be released.* In many areas of life an important moment comes between a phase of preparation and building, and another phase of practical use. When the sluices are finally opened on a new dam, the water that has been piling up behind it is released to drive the turbines and produce electricity. When a couple have saved up for long enough they may buy a car, or put a deposit on a new house. Often this moment is marked by some kind of ceremony; a notable person turns up to open a hospital, launch a ship, or drive the first car down a motorway. There is something rather important about this transition from preparing a thing to actually using it.

It is sometimes not realised that faith needs to be released in the same way. A person's growing conviction that he should believe and repent is finally released when he makes a public commitment, or perhaps is baptised. Also with healing, the faith of the person prayed for and the faith of the person praying may be released in some symbolic act such as the laying on of hands, or the touching of a prayer cloth. This happened to the woman in Luke (8. 43–48) whose faith needed the release of physical contact with Jesus' garment. It wasn't that the clothes Jesus was wearing had somehow come to be charged with his healing power. If the woman's faith had depended on touching his footprints much the same thing would have happened – he would have felt the virtue going out of him, and turned. Even more strange is the instance of sick people being healed by the passing of Peter's shadow (Acts 5:12–16). This was not, as it might appear, a superstitious act; their faith simply needed that moment of release to make it effective.

What constitutes a release for us today will vary. For some it will be the laying on of hands, for others an emotional experience that allows them to drop their inhibitions and tensions and receive healing. For everyone there is an experience, a certain moment or kind of moment, that will focus their faith in such a way that it becomes fully effective. How it might happen is suggested by the story told in the Gospel of John about the man who had been ill for thirty-eight years and waited for healing by the pool of Bethesda. He had faith, there was no doubt about that. But the release of that faith depended on the local belief that when an angel came down and disturbed the water of the pool, only the first man to reach the water's edge would be healed; and being lame, this man was always pipped to the post by someone more mobile than he was.

Jesus did two things. He first asked the man if he wanted to be made whole, and then, rather than override his faith, gave him another means of releasing it. Strangely, the man did not say yes to the first question; in effect he replied, 'I can't be healed because I can't walk and I've got no one to help me.' He had become obsessed with his disability and the strictures it imposed on him. But Jesus simply broke through all that. 'You can't use your faith that way,' he was saying. 'But now if you want I'll give you a new way to use it.' Presented with this new opportunity for the release of faith the man stood up, rolled up his pallet, and was healed.

It is possible for a person to accumulate the faith necessary for healing, and yet miss out for want of an opportunity for its release. Taking crusades and laying hands on the sick is one way of meeting this need and allowing faith to do its work – or perhaps I should say, allowing faith to allow the Spirit to do his work. When I ask a man to leave his seat at a meeting and join a queue for healing faith can be released by an action of the will. That does not mean that healing takes place through will-power, any more than it is will-power debiting your account when you sign a cheque. In both cases you undertake a simple action to signify your desire that a certain thing should take place. Somebody else does the rest. The method has the double effect of confirming a person's desire for healing, and providing a special moment in which their faith may be released.

Power to heal

There is no doubt whatever in my mind that God is ready and willing to heal. A verse from Paul's letter to the Ephesians sums it up marvellously, when he commits them to 'him that is able to do exceedingly abundantly above all that we ask or think' (Eph. 3:20). Like fillings in a monster hamburger Paul lays up the superlatives until it is almost too big to get your mouth round it. If God did simply all we asked or thought he would be well occupied and we would see some pretty astounding miracles. But he goes beyond that, and not just once, but three times. God acts *above* our thoughts and expectations, *abundantly above* them, then *exceedingly abundantly above* them. There was no single word in the Greek language Paul could get his hands on that expressed adequately the way we could be swamped with God's blessing.

But he adds one qualification. Though the fact that God is able to do these things is beyond question, how far he does them is determined, as the next phrase says, 'according to the power that worketh in us' (Eph. 3:20). My reading of that says God is limited, by the rules he has himself laid down, to work within the bounds of our faith. He never forces his will on us, even for our blessing. The amount of benefit we derive from the reservoir of divine love is in proportion to our turning of the taps. If our faith is such that we trust God without reservation, then we can have all our baths and washbasins overflowing and start a river of living water flowing down the street; if our faith is grudging and hedged about with conditions, then it will hardly be surprising if we fail to get what we ask for.

The nurturing of faith is therefore an important part of the healing ministry, whether you are praying or being prayed for. In the final analysis your right to healing does not depend on your membership of a lively church, the godliness or spirituality of your minister, or the faith of your friends. God is interested in you personally, not the various little strings you can pull. And it seems to be the case (though, because faith is within us, I cannot prove it) that healing will not occur in a person whose heart has no spark of repentance or faith, be it ever so small and perhaps scarcely realised. Even Jesus was unable to do miracles in places where faith dwindled (cf Matt. 13:58).

At the same time there is ample evidence to suggest that healing can be helped by the faith of those around us. When the palsied man's four friends let him down in front of Jesus through the roof of the Galilean house, it wasn't the sick man's faith Jesus commended, but theirs (Mark 2:5). In my own experience I have often seen people saved or healed who before they heard the gospel had no knowledge of God, let alone faith in him. One of them, Benny, worked as a bouncer in a Staffordshire night club, and wouldn't have come to a meeting at all without the persuasion of his wife. She wasn't a Christian, but she had diabetes, and so when she got a leaflet through the door one day she was determined to attend the crusade. Benny wasn't impressed; he thought all this healing business was a con trick. But when he made the excuse that he could not take her because the crusade, being at night, interfered with his work, she quickly told him that the meeting began at seven-thirty, and since he didn't begin work until nine there was no reason he shouldn't go. Both of them were saved, and Benny's wife has never suffered from diabetes since. What they themselves lacked in faith was made up by the expectant faith of the others at the meeting – and it was effective.

This is encouraging because it means, among other things, that a lively Christian congregation can provide a context in which even the most unlikely sinners may find salvation and healing. And very often, as with Paul, it is the toughest sinners who make the greatest saints. I am fond of a story about a famous restaurant, renowned for its expensive decor, where a young man once tripped over and emptied the content of his coffee cup over one of the walls. Understandably the manager was furious. Not only was the stain large, it was also in a very prominent place. Help, however, was at hand. Another young man who had been sitting at a nearby table laid aside his napkin and came forward holding in his hand a small metal box. He gently persuaded the manager to let him work on the stain, then set to with paint and brushes, joining the rough edges together into a single, smooth form. In a short time there emerged from the awful stain a startlingly beautiful picture of a highland deer. The manager was delighted, not least because its fame spread and soon people were eating in the restaurant just to see the painting on the wall. And the artist? That was Landseer, later to become one of the finest watercolour painters of wildlife in the world.

Nevertheless

If coffee stains could think, they would probably not rate very highly their chances of turning into masterpieces. Most of them would be right. And that is the way many people feel about their healing – that in spite of all this talk about trusting God and releasing faith, it just doesn't seem very likely that diabetes, cancer, arthritis or blindness is really going to go away. Who can imagine a miracle like that, still less trust God with a realistic expectation that it will happen?

If that is the way you feel, then rest assured you are not the first person to feel it. All of us do at some time or another, and in fact it is a useful, down-to-earth attitude applicable to a great number of situations, not just healing. We generally call it *realism*. It stops us running for buses that we've already missed, and putting vast sums of money on a horse with long odds and short legs. There's no point in kidding yourself, we sometimes say – you have to be realistic.

Unfortunately realism in God's vocabulary is a relative term. If the truth be told, God has devoted a great deal of energy in the past to projects we would see as completely futile. Some of his best include building large boats in the desert, (Gen. 5:14) demolishing walls by walking round them with trumpets, (Josh. 6:20) getting a ninety year old woman to give birth, (Gen. 17:17–19) and raising corpses from the dead (John 11:44)–none of them remotely realistic in the orthodox sense. Nonetheless they all worked. It is this sort of realism that God expects his people to have; that is, one that is based on God's proven track record and not what day to day experience seems to say is true. Someone who puts aside his despair and acts, just for a moment, on God's realism, will see a miracle.

Look at Peter toiling away at his fishing in Luke 5. He came back to land without so much as a sardine to find a preacher standing on his strip of shoreline; worse still, the preacher had the audacity to borrow Peter's boat as a pulpit while he spoke to the crowds on the beach, and then, by way of thanks, offered some unsolicited advice on how Peter should be plying his trade. 'Launch out into the deep, and let down your nets for a draught' (Luke 5:4).

Peter, who fancied himself as a bit of an old salt, wasn't overjoyed to hear a landlubber giving him orders. It was sheer effrontery for an upstart preacher to think he knew more about fishing than a seasoned professional, and the professional approach after a whole night of unsuccessful fishing was to cut your losses and go home for breakfast. On the other hand, Jesus clearly wasn't just any preacher, and there was something about the way he spoke that made Peter mellow his reply, and half way through it actually change his mind: 'Master, we have toiled all the night and have taken nothing: nevertheless at thy word I will let down the net.'

The pivotal word is *nevertheless.* All Peter's professional instincts told him that the realistic thing was to stay right where he was and tell Jesus to mind his own business. He was tired, the fish hadn't bitten, and the crowd had probably scared them away by now anyway. *Nevertheless* that little spark of faith goaded him into action. He would do it in spite of his own better judgment, on the strength of Jesus' word. He believed, and he acted – and that was enough. This small motion of the will was just strong enough to make him get back into the boat, push off from the land and toss in his net. From there the miracle took over: 'When they had done this, they enclosed a great multitude of fishes, and their net break . . . ' (Luke 5:6).

You will be able to think of all sorts of good and realistic reasons not to seek God for healing. There's no proof it works. You've had a heavy day at work and there are lots of odd jobs to be caught up on at home. Your illness has been getting progressively worse for the last two years, and there's no real hope of getting better. In fact it is the doctor's stated opinion that unless you have another operation there is no possibility even of staying the decline where it is. No one you've ever heard of has been healed, and anyway you were prayed for a long time ago, and nothing happened. Going to a meeting, being prayed for, simply isn't realistic.

Nevertheless . . .

7: Ways and Means

Our great need is a band who will bear witness to the truth of Christ . . . till health steps back into the nation.

Archbishop William Coggan

In the last two chapters we have outlined two great principles of healing: the word of God, and faith. We have pictured the word of God as a vast reservoir that is able to provide for the needs of every individual, and faith as the turning of a tap which brings the flow of healing into our lives. By extension of the same analogy, this chapter is about taps. What different kinds of tap are linked to this reservoir of healing power? What means has God ordained for effecting healing among his people? There are many; and once again it is vital to base our answers not in experience, but on the Bible. This is our sole reliable guide in the practice of healing, and the touchstone by which we may recognise an authentic ministry from a specious one – it is, after all, important to distinguish a cold water tap from a petrol pump.

So what does Scripture teach us about 'taps'?

Better than cure

Stopping yourself getting a disease in the first place isn't quite the same as having it healed; and discussing prevention here may seem to many readers like those lectures well meaning parents give about 'looking where you're going' to children with grazed knees. I am going to justify it though on the same grounds as normal preventative medicine: that since the object of healing is health it is better to stay healthy than to get sick and need to be healed. As Bryn Jones has put it, 'Abundant health is not finding victory, but living in it; not just being healed, but living in health.' The writer of Psalm 43 described God as 'the health of my countenance' (Ps. 43:5 KJV), an experience that must have been enjoyed by Moses, who when he died at the age of one hundred and twenty was still in perfect health: 'His eye was not dim, nor his natural force abated' (Deut. 34:7).

In the last few years a lot of attention has been given to the business of looking after the body. Everywhere you go you'll find an advertisement or a poster telling you to eat more fibre, play more squash, jog more miles or drink less beer. Most margarine manufacturers seem to agree that butter will kill you, and no self-respecting toothpaste tube appears on the pharmacy shelves without some reference to fluoride and plaque on the cover. Even smoking is less popular than it used to be, as more and more studies confirm its connection with cardiovascular disease and cancer.

All this publicity for health is good. But it is sometimes rather technical, with the result that many people only change their habits when habit-changing becomes a trend. Take the butter-or-margarine problem. Do you know what *polyunsaturates* are? Would you know one if you saw it on the street? I wouldn't. If Joe Bloggs hadn't told me over the garden fence last week that since he's used polyunsaturated margarine his weight's gone right down, I'd never even have tried it. I behave like this (and probably you do too) because human beings are most likely to trust what they can understand. The molecular structure of fat means nothing to me; on the other hand, the argument that eating the right margarine might keep my weight down is very persuasive. Perhaps the day will come when we are all bright enough to take in the science behind our health; but it is interesting that the Bible does not make this assumption. It just gives us straightforward instructions which, if we follow them, will keep us fit. And very often these instructions are what the scientists are now telling us to do as a result of their own complicated investigations.

Here then is a checklist of biblical hints for health:

(1) Rest
If God put his feet up after creating the world we would be well advised to do the same thing at the end of the working week. In fact rest on the seventh day is prescribed in the Ten Commandments (Exod. 20:8–11). There should be one day in seven when we can forget the stresses and problems of life and relax. If this means watching a movie on the television or taking the kids out to the forest that's fine; but it would be even better if we were able to relax in Christian worship, so that as Jesus withdrew into the wilderness to pray we could find rest and recuperation in praise and fellowship with other Christians. It is very important for effective living and ministry, as well as preventing illness, that we do not overwork ourselves, or allow ourselves to be overworked by the laziness of others around us. 'Graveyards,' the saying goes, 'are full of indispensible people.'

(2) Diet
We have a peculiar habit of eating at the wrong times. When we've just had a good supper we very often go to the cupboard and down a couple of biscuits for good measure; and if we're out in the garden digging vegetables we may pass over a meal because it's too much bother to clean up, and anyway it would 'probably do us good to go without'. This kind of sporadic eating bears no relation to our bodily needs. We should eat when we need to, not when we happen to have time, and certainly not because we feel bored or peckish – that road will lead us to a dependence on food that amounts to a worship of our own bellies (cf. Phil. 3:19). Moreover, psychologists tell us that overeating is itself a symptom of another condition – inadequacy, boredom, anger, frustration, or simple indiscipline. This will need to be sorted out if we are to obey Paul's instruction to honour God with our bodies. So watch that late night snacking! On the other hand, when

we require food we should – unless we have some definite reason – take it. When Jesus raised Jairus' daughter from the dead he didn't send her out on the terrace to wave at the crowds; he made sure she was fed. Excess and deficiency of food both lead to ill-health, and it will do us a lot of good to heed the biblical maxim, 'moderation in all things'. This includes, of course, having food not just in the correct quantities, but also of the right sort, and here the key is variety. God didn't provide such a wealth of food in the world to have us get along on a diet of beer and chips.

(3) Exercise

Unfortunately Paul is reported by the Authorised Version as saying 'Bodily exercise profiteth little' (1 Tim. 4:8). He was comparing it with spiritual exercise, which in his opinion was a far more worthwhile activity; but if Paul didn't go out every morning for a six o'clock jog, he wasn't quite as down on physical exercise as the Authorised Version suggests. A better translation runs, 'Physical training is of some value . . . ' (NIV). The Old Testament corroborates this implicitly with its observation that 'the slothful man roasteth not that which he took in hunting' (Prov. 11:27). That no more direct comment is made on physical exercise in Scripture perhaps reflects the difference between the ancient world and the modern. In biblical times there were far fewer pen-pushing jobs, which meant that most of the population got quite enough exercise without having to resort to Jane Fonda work-outs. Having, myself, a job that is typically modern in that it involves no great physical exertion, I try to get in between one and two miles of walking (or stately trotting) every day.

(4) Cleanliness

This is not as close to godliness as the proverb suggests, but there is a strong tradition of ritual cleansing in the Law of the Old Testament (cf. Lev. 15) which served to emphasise the Israelites' special position before God, 'That ye may put difference between holy and unholy, and between unclean and clean.' (Lev. 10:10). Because this had a religious rather than a scientific basis we do not need to observe the Old Testament Law in its entirety – not that we are likely, anyway, to be offered a bowl of pelican and lapwing stew (Lev. 11:18, 19) or to enter a house with a case of leprosy (Lev. 14:36). What we do need to recognise, though, is how these observances cultivated the habit of personal cleanliness in the Israelites, and that consequently physical and spiritual cleanness came to mirror one another. When James wrote at a later time, 'Cleanse your hands, ye sinners,' he would have been writing in a culture for which the washing of the hands had also the purpose of removing dirt. Conversely, the physical washing of the disciples' feet (John 13:10) is understood to have a spiritual significance. From this point of view it appears that personal cleanliness runs parallel to righteous behaviour as a way of glorifying God in our bodies, which are the temple of God (1 Cor. 6:22).

(5) Avoiding risks

Christians are not supernaturally protected from illness. Paul suffered from the cold when he was in gaol, and asked Timothy in his first letter to bring the cloak he had left behind at Troas. That means that if we decide to go out in the rain without an overcoat we will have no one to blame but ourselves if we end up in bed with the flu. Of course there have been times when, rain or no rain, Christians have been obliged to leave their overcoats behind. The early African missionaries believed risk to be part of their calling, and suffered terribly with tropical diseases while propagating the gospel. At the same time it was incumbent upon them to use what little knowledge they had to protect themselves; and as knowledge increases so the preventative measures available to us multiply. Travelling abroad I still try to boil my water, take all the necessary inoculations before I go, and after a hot evening's work in a crusade meeting always bathe or shower and dry down with a towel.

(6) Being positive

Stress has been identified as one of the major contributing factors in modern illness. It is in part a reaction to the age we live in; often we work too hard and worry too much over things going wrong. It isn't always helpful, either, to be told to calm down or take things easy. As any insomniac will tell you, we can rest our bodies far more easily than our minds. This is why the biblical solution is one of transferring anxiety, 'Casting all your care upon him; for he careth for you' (1 Pet. 5:7). We can reduce stress by realising that God is in charge of our lives. The success of next week's business meeting doesn't only depend on us – it is in the hands of God. Understanding this we are able to pray and think positively without being dominated by fear of disaster or resentment over failure. God cares for us.

God's chosen fast

Fasting isn't what we first think of in connection with healing, but the scriptural warrant for using it is very strong. In its simplest form fasting means abstaining from food for spiritual purposes, and as such has been used not only by Christ and his followers but by many of the world's religions. A fast doesn't have to be total – many who fast regularly recommend drinking milk or orange juice as well as water; in length it may vary from a single missed meal to several days, perhaps as many as forty, though long fasts of this sort should only be done with practice and great care. Moses, David, Elijah, Ezra and Daniel are all said to have fasted, either in repentance, or petition, or for spiritual strength, (see Ezra 10:6; Esther 4:16; Dan. 10:3) and their example has been followed by innumerable Christians of the modern era, including Calvin, Luther, Knox, Finney, Brainerd, and John Wesley, who fasted every Friday his whole life through.

But fasting is not always a matter of going without food. Arthur Wallace hit on the essence of the discipline when he described it as an abstinence from 'anything that hinders our communion with God.' In this sense fasting is a form of self-denial. In the words of Andrew Murray, 'Fasting helps us to express and confirm . . . that we are ready to sacrifice anything to attain what we seek for the Kingdom of God!' Just how helpful Jesus expected it to be is shown by his own fasting and the assumption that his disciples would do it as a matter of course. His teaching on the subject commences with not 'If you ever feel like fasting . . . ' but 'When ye fast . . . '

Fasting may be undertaken for a variety of reasons. Paul fasted in the face of his own need when he was struck with blindness on the Damascus Road (Acts 9:9). Joel, on the other hand, proclaimed a fast on behalf of the nation. 'Blow the trumpet in Zion, sanctify a fast . . . let them say, "Spare thy people, O Lord"' (Joel 2:15, 17). In general fasting is a way of clearing the lines between God and his people; a way, if you like, of bypassing the taps and boring right into the mains. 'This kind,' said Jesus of a particularly resistant demon, 'goeth not out but by prayer and fasting' (Matt. 17:21). 'So we fasted and besought out God for this: and he was intreated of us,' said Ezra, mindful of the dangers awaiting the tiny band of Jews going back to rebuild Jerusalem.

In my opinion healing would be more frequent and more complete if both preachers and congregation were prepared to seek God seriously through the discipline of fasting. Certainly it cannot be left only to those with the gift of healing. I remember one occasion when I was asked to pray for a woman too ill to attend the crusade. As I entered her room I knew intuitively that she held out no hope of being healed, and saw me as another poor preacher being wheeled on to do something that was self-evidently impossible. So the first thing I said to her was this: 'Have you prepared for my coming to pray for you?' The expression on her face told me this was the last thing she'd thought of doing. 'In that case,' I went on, 'I'll come back another day when you have prayed and fasted, and you're ready for God's servant to minister to you.' When I returned the following week she had done exactly as I'd said, and she was healed immediately.

'Is not this the fast that I have chosen . . . to let the oppressed go free?' (Isa. 58:6).

He touched me

In France during the Middle Ages the disease scrofula is said to have been cured by the touch of a king, and for that reason to have acquired the name the *King's Evil.* Touching was introduced in England by Edward the Confessor and in the time of Henry VII took the form of a ceremony in which gold coins were dispensed to the sufferers. It reached its height under Charles II who during his life touched one hundred thousand victims of scrofula (sometimes in crowds so large that people were trampled to death). It declined under the influence of a rather sceptical William III, and was carried out for the last time by Queen Anne – without success – in 1712.

Whether this treatment ever worked no one knows. What we do know is that Jesus used the method of touching, or 'laying on of hands', and that through it a great number of sick people were made whole. Luke records the following instance: 'A man full of leprosy . . . seeing Jesus fell on his face and besought him, saying, "Lord, if thou wilt, thou canst make me clean." And he put forth his hand, and touched him, saying, "I will; be thou clean." And immediately the leprosy departed from him' (Luke 5:12, 13).

There is nothing special about the action itself. Jesus' touching appears to have been no more than a brief physical contact, and although there is evidence that among his disciples the action became slightly more formal (cf. 1 Tim. 4:14; 5:22), the difference is a matter of detail. The touch employed by Christians in the ministry of healing isn't osteopathy, or manipulation; still less is it some kind of bizarre channelling of the life force, applied as a doctor might go about the laser treatment of a cancer. It is simply a touch – releasing faith, symbolising through a human touch the touch of God himself. But it is effective, and has brought healing to hundreds of thousands. As the hymnwriter says,

'Thy touch hath still its ancient power;
  No work from Thee can fruitless fall;
Hear in this solemn evening hour,
  And in thy mercy heal us all.'

Besides having the greatest Scriptural precedent, laying on of hands is the method most commonly used by healers and evangelists today. It is straightforward and fast – important considerations for the Christian minister who is required to be an instrument of healing to perhaps five hundred people in a single night. He cannot enter deeply into each individual case, or use an elaborate ritual or prayer. Laying on of hands brings personal contact without losing that due sense of gravity associated with approaching the King of kings for healing.

To illustrate its use I could pick on an almost inexhaustible supply of examples. Many of them are contained in my first book, *Healing Revolution*. The one that springs to mind here happened during a tour of Malaysia, where I had the joy of ministering in some very remote villages and often found myself preaching Christ when the temperature was a hundred degrees in the shade. I made a point of laying hands on everyone who requested it, whether they were Buddhists, Hindus, Sikhs or Christians. The testimony of one man, Mr Valayudan, reached me long afterwards:

'I want to thank God for saving and healing me. I was suffering from severe heart trouble. I could not eat or do simple things for myself, and even the doctors at Segamat Hospital gave me no hope.

As I could not work, an Indian Assembly of God pastor came to pray with me, and he shared Jesus with me. I accepted Christ as my personal Saviour, and later I was asked by the pastor to come to one of the village meetings of Pastor Melvin Banks from England.

They took me to a great hall. To see the crowds of sick people was most moving, all gathered together. Pastor Banks prayed with me, and laid hands upon me in Jesus' name. Before this I could hardly talk, I was so sick. But now my speech is normal, I can eat, I can walk up and down stairs, and I have no pain . . . '

Oil of gladness

'Is any sick among you?' asked James in his epistle. 'Let him call for the elders of the church and let them pray over him, anointing him with oil in the name of the Lord. And the prayer of faith shall save the sick, and the Lord shall raise him up, and if he have committed sins, they shall be forgiven him' (Jam. 5:14, 15).

Oil is mentioned throughout the Scriptures. We read in Leviticus that Moses 'poured the anointing oil on Aaron's head, and anointed him, to sanctify him' (Lev. 8:12). Later, when Samuel wished to signify that God had chosen Saul as king, the oil was used again–this time with a warning, for when the Spirit fell on him Saul would be 'turned into another man' (1 Sam. 10:6). Similarly with the anointing of Saul's successor, David, on whom 'The Spirit of the Lord came . . . from that day forward' (1 Sam. 16:13). Both references indicate that to be anointed with oil was to be set aside for a special purpose and, more especially, to receive the gift of the Holy Spirit.

This is probably why James, writing in the New Testament, gives the anointing a ceremonial air that we do not find in descriptions of the laying on of hands. As the prophets anointed in the Old Testament, so, in the church, anointing is cited as a special responsibility of the elders. Nor is this a blessing to be conferred indiscriminately; we have no record of Gentiles being anointed under the Old Covenant, and the disciples sent out by Jesus, according to Mark given power to heal through anointing with oil, are in the parallel account in Matthew's Gospel forbidden to preach to any but the lost sheep of the house of Israel. 'In this particular form of institutional healing,' says Aaron Linford, 'there is no scriptural warrant for anointing unbelievers.'

So why, if you are a Christian, should you choose to be anointed with oil and not simply touched in the way you might have been by Jesus? To some extent it is a decision of conscience. Touching and anointing are in themselves symbolic, and there is no reason to suppose that by being anointed with oil you are getting a five-star treatment. It does, however, have particular associations and emphases that may be more significant and helpful for certain people. One, it reminds us strongly that we are healed through the action of the Holy Spirit. Two, it makes a clear division between our past of sickness and disobedience, and the new life of health and spiritual wholeness. And three, it acts as a reminder of the 'Royal Seal' God places on our healing, in the same way as David was anointed not just to show he would one day be king, but to indicate under whose authority he would be granted to rule.

One last, and reassuring point about anointing with oil is that we are not bound to follow Moses' example and pour on so much that it runs down over the recipient's beard, jersey and clean shirt. A touch with the fingertip is quite enough – it's oil we're dealing with, not hair cream.

Hankies and aprons

The Bible mentions these as a means of healing only once, but the reference is explicit. 'God wrought special miracles by the hands of Paul: so that from his body were brought unto the sick handkerchiefs or aprons, and the diseases departed from them, and the evil spirits went out of them' (Acts 19:11, 12).

It is actually a rather useful clause in God's agreement about healing, because a great many people who would like to attend a meeting will never be able to get there, and any

Christian gifted in healing will be limited in the number of house calls he can make. For this reason, and because I believe that whatever the Bible allows is legitimate practice today, our office sends out around four thousand hankies every year. We even received a request a few months ago from a group of Arabs in the Jordanian desert! Occasionally we get a reply to tell of a healing by this means – a notable one coming from a lady on the Isle of Wight who had been in and out of hospital for five years, and within four days of having a handkerchief laid on her was completely recovered.

The question arises, of course, if hankies are allowed, why not bracelets, photographs, string vests and goodness knows what else? In fact we do sometimes get letters asking for a blessing on various trinkets, and these are invariably returned along with a handkerchief I have prayed over and a personal letter explaining that although in principle you may as well pray over a piece of jewellery as an apron or handkerchief, the latter are in fact the only items specifically allowed by Scripture. If this were not the case there would soon be a proliferation of 'holy' items going through the post and we would be back once again with the saints' nail parings. With this means of healing, more than any other, it needs to be emphasised that the cloth carries no special properties; it is not magic, nor is its use superstitious. The handkerchief acts to release faith, to bring about the moment of healing that would otherwise have occurred through another means like the laying on of hands.

The exorcist

Exorcism, or deliverance, is like other means of healing in that it acts as a 'tap' for the release of God's healing power. But it is only applicable to certain kinds of illness, namely those which result from the direct and not the general activity of Satan and demonic forces. Distinguishing the two isn't always easy, and a proper treatment of the topic would require more space than we can afford here. Briefly, some demoniacs exhibit clear symptoms of affliction with evil spirits, while others behave much as they would under emotional or psychological strain. Even ordinary physical ailments can be caused by demonic activity. This is why the gift of discernment of spirits is so important in the ministry of deliverance.

There are two mistakes a Christian can make in the area of exorcism. One is to be sceptical and insist that any illness, physical or psychiatric, can be explained through conventional medicine. This point of view simply doesn't square with Scripture. The devil is mentioned over one hundred and twenty times in the Bible, demons twenty-five times. The Apostle John left no doubt that Jesus was manifested not to improve on current philosophical thinking but to 'destroy the works of the Devil' (1 John 3:8) and Jesus himself made a clear distinction between the sick (on whom he generally laid hands) and the possessed (whom he exorcised). If we think that reports like these are only wild stories disclaimed by later, more cool-headed Christians, we must still account for Paul's assertion that 'we wrestle not against flesh and blood, but against the rulers of the darkness of this world, against spiritual wickedness in high places' (Eph. 6:12). I myself have ministered to a large number of people afflicted with demons, and am convinced that they would never have recovered from their illnesses without this particular form of prayer.

But there is another mistake to be made, and that is to jump in with both feet and to do it yourself. That, in my opinion, is extremely dangerous both for the person praying and the person prayed for; it is like going in to repair high tension power cables without having the slightest idea how electricity works. I don't mean that Christians are always subject to the forces of Satan. But it is the experienced hunter who is most likely to kill the tiger, not the amateur marksman who has spent his life shooting at card targets. Exorcism is quite simply a specialist ministry.

A last point is on the sort of people who may be affected by illness of this kind. Personally I don't think it necessary to conclude that a sufferer is exceptionally wicked or backslidden, although past association with the occult is very often a contributary factor. An enormous number of people suffer from illness of the mind – in fact they occupy about sixty per cent of hospital beds in Britain. Some of them suffer violent depressions and insanity, others have milder disorders associated with tension, frustration and anxiety. Often these conditions have nothing to do with the Devil, but all of them *can* be caused by evil spirits, and when a particular case is spotted exorcism will be necessary to overcome and remove them.

Happiness heals

'A merry heart doeth good like a medicine, but a broken spirit drieth the bones' (Prov. 17:22).

Joy is never very far away from the Christian soul. 'The joy of the Lord is your strength,' said Nehemiah to the returned exiles, in one of four hundred biblical references to the word. John Wesley was quite right to say 'holiness is happiness'; Jesus identified joy as the purpose of petitionary prayer 'Ask and ye shall receive, that your joy may be full' (John 16:24) and C. S. Lewis, who titled the story of his conversion *Surprised by Joy*, revealed its place in the consummation of history: 'Pain and pleasure sink almost out of sight; there is joy . . . incomparable with the sufferings of the present.'

This last quotation gives something away, though. Joy in the biblical sense is not just elation or a feeling of being at one with the world. It is bigger than that, so big in fact that only God is large enough to contain it and it is to him that we must go if we want to discover it. It is the joy of the *Lord*. A lot of people go wrong here because they think the joy of the Lord is exactly the same as all the other joy they have in life – through children, love or success. These do bring great joy, but they are infinitely inferior to God's joy, just as his love, his fatherhood and his success so far outdistance ours. And when we go to worship in a church it is not ordinary joy we will find there – a dull sermon will soon put paid to that!—but the joy that leads us on to God's presence as the warm light of a window leads us to the front door.

This joy we begin to discover in praise, and in both together we discover healing. I have known many sick people healed through praise and joy long before I get to lay hands on them; sometimes there are so many that I ask them to stand up and give testimony before the healing time begins. Joy and praise act as a means of healing every bit as effective as touching or anointing with oil. One reason is that praise opens up a person's heart to the presence of God in a way that quiet prayer or discussion may not do. Somehow it digs right through our minds to the emotions and the spirit, flattening our inhibitions and triggering all sorts of things that are beyond our conscious control but which need to be touched before healing can take place.

But if praise brings us into the presence of God, it also brings God's presence to us. The psalmist describes God as 'thou that inhabitest the praises of Israel' (Ps. 22:3). In other words the praise and joy of his people brings God near to them, shortens, if you like, the distance between the reservoir and the tap. It thus strengthens prayer, sets up the right atmosphere for faith to be effective and for healing to take place; indeed it is often sufficient on its own to bring about a miracle.

Sometimes I come home from a big crusade service very exhausted. I take a bath ('wash off the fellowship', as one old pentecostal preacher put it!) then I sit down in front of the fire with my dressing gown on and just *laugh*. I laugh with happiness and praise for the way Satan has been routed, so many people have been set free, so much sickness and suffering has gone, and so many souls have been truly converted. I know the kingdom of God has been advanced a little further, and that fills me with joy. And the joy always brings with it recovery, refreshment and healing.

I am sure that living in the joy of the Lord is one of the best things you can do for a healthy body and a happy life—but that leads us on to the final part of this chapter.

Live long in the land

'Honour thy father and mother,' wrote Paul '(which is the first commandment with promise), that it may be well with thee, and thou mayest live long on the earth' (Eph. 6: 2,3).

In a way this brings us back to where we started, for the commandment quoted by Paul here is one of the many passages in Scripture that relate health and long life to holy and obedient living. 'The angel of the Lord encampeth about them that fear him, and delivereth them' (Ps. 34:7). 'The fear of the Lord is the beginning of wisdom: and the knowledge of the holy is understanding; for by me thy days shall be multiplied, and the years of thy life shall be increased' (Prov. 9:10, 11). 'They that wait upon the Lord shall renew their strength' (Isa. 40:31). 'Keep my commandments: for length of days, and long life, and peace, shall they add to thee' (Prov. 3:1, 2).

There is a clear promise in the Bible that if we will keep busy for God, remember his laws and words and not break them, then we will live long on the earth and enjoy vigour and health. But this lays two responsibilities on us. One, to obey God's commandments, and two, to believe in faith his promise to keep us in life and health. The first is clear enough; the second is a matter of expectation, of being positive in the way I outlined earlier – of positively thinking of freedom from disease, soundness in body, release from painful memories. God wants his children to be hale and fit; he rejoices to see a long life wisely spent. He loves grand-parents!

If you conduct yourself in obedience and faithful anticipation of a full and healthy life, then, as the writer of Proverbs put it, 'Thine expectation shall not be cut off' (Prov. 23:18).

8: The Doctor and Death

And the leaves of the tree were for the healing of the nations
St John

Some readers may feel that one very important means of divine healing was omitted in the last chapter. 'Isn't it true,' they will ask, 'that hundreds of unseen and unacknowledged miracles take place every day through the skill of medical doctors?' They are not diluting the term 'miracle'. There are, of course, many things that are miraculous in the more general sense of 'wonderful' or 'unexpected'; but it is a serious question whether God works through doctors to bring about healing in a way that is parallel to miracles of the divine healing ministry.

This is one issue I want to deal with now. But I also want to touch on another important problem connected with healing – that of death. It is true for all of us – as it was true for all the believers in the Bible except Enoch and Elijah – that however healthy a life we lead there will come a day when the mortal body wears out and we have to die. Even Lazarus whom Jesus called back through the gates of death presumably had to pass through them again in the end. For this reason our understanding of death is crucial to the healing gift. We have to ask whether healing makes any sense in a universe ruled by death, and in what way we as Christians are meant to have power over it.

The beloved physician

The relationship between orthodox medicine and divine healing hangs on our definition of illness, specifically whether we see it as an affliction brought on by Satan or by God. I remember addressing a meeting of church ministers in a Cheshire town where I was soon to begin a three week mission. One member voiced quite strongly his opinion that illness came by the will of God, and that the correct response, far from seeking divine healing, was to suffer in the belief that God was either chastising us for sin, or bringing us to a higher state of moral perfection. When he'd finished I asked him what he did when he was sick. 'I go to the doctor,' he replied. By the look of him he'd never had a day's serious illness in his life. I said, 'Well, if what you say is true, when you are ill you shouldn't even be going to the doctor. God's will is God's will. The moment you go to a surgery with the flu you're disobeying him!

That is the logical conclusion of the argument that illness comes by the will of God. You lie down and take whatever comes, in the same way as a Muslim accepts personal calamity as the will of Allah. But things look very different if you view illness as a work of the Devil, for then any efforts human beings make to alleviate its effects will be, to some extent or another, fighting on God's side. Doctors fall into the same category as the men the disciple John reported to Jesus: 'Master, we saw one casting out devils in thy name; and we forbad him, because he followeth not with us. And Jesus said unto him, "Forbid him not: for he that is not against us is for us"' (Luke 9:49, 50). This is not the same as saying all doctors are Christians. But most medical practice is a 'good work' of the sort Jesus commended in his story of the Good Samaritan. Doctors who are also Christian believers would probably go further and say that medical treatment, for all the complex skills that go with it nowadays, is an invitation for God, the real healer, to carry out his job. As a famous missionary doctor once said, 'I bind the patient's wounds, but God heals him.'

There is a point, though, at which the doctor and the Christian healer must part company, and this is where medical procedures are clearly immoral. Abortion, for instance, can never be permitted by Christians because it involves the taking of a human life. Supplying teenagers with contraceptives can only have the effect of encouraging permissive behaviour, and this in turn, as I have seen repeatedly in counselling, will distort a young person's sense of values and reduce his or her chance of enjoying a lasting and happy marriage. Surrogate motherhood – the bearing of a child by one woman for another – has no biblical justification, and sperm donation seems to me to be simply adultery by proxy. I believe that these practices, which have been fully backed or at least unofficially supported by doctors, are smears on the reputation of a profession that otherwise works in accordance with God's laws and in the spirit of charity and peace.

But even medicine rightly used has its limitations. As soon as a person is diagnosed as having cancer he will want to know whether it is benign or malignant, because benign tumours can usually be removed whereas malignant ones are more serious. Very many diseases can still only be partially treated, or retarded. That is why such a lot of people come to healing crusades; in a recent survey taken at one of my meetings ninety-nine percent of those interviewed had been declared medically incurable. I don't think I would be slandering the medical profession if I said that many today find themselves in the same position as the Jewish woman Jesus healed, who 'had suffered many things of many physicians, and had spent all that she had, and was nothing bettered, but rather grew worse' (Mark 5:26).

To be fair, divine healing has its critics too. One hears from time to time reports of people, perhaps with multiple sclerosis, who after being encouraged to discard their crutches and walk, soon find themselves far worse off than they were before. I can only say that so far as I am aware this has not occurred with any of the half million people I have prayed for. If I am right, then the credit is certainly due to balanced teaching and careful prayer governed by the wisdom of God. I do not urge anyone to discontinue medical treatment as an expression of faith, though this may sometimes be the right thing to do and I would not hold anyone back if they were determined to do it. As Paul said, 'Let every man be fully persuaded in his own mind' (Rom 14:5). What I do very often tell a sick person to do is to return to their clinic and obtain a clean bill of health. Official confirmations of healing are a marvellous witness and have happened thousands of times. Not long ago a lady in Yorkshire who had suffered from polio went back to hospital to have her file closed with the words 'Healed by prayer'!

A very few Christians believe that it is wrong to have any dealings whatever with secular medicine. They are fond of quoting the passage about King Asa, who with his diseased feet 'sought not to the Lord, but to the physicians', and promptly died. The point, of course, is not that he went to the physicians, but that he refused to go to God. Had he lived in an age of more proficient medicine God might have sent him to the physician anyway, content that he had at least had the decency and faith to consult him. As it was, by relying on his pet quacks Asa was signing his own death warrant. They didn't know what was wrong with him and God wasn't giving away any clues.

Often, though, God will work directly through the skill of doctors. A survey in the *Practitioner* some time ago compared two groups of incurable cancer patients, one of which received constant and personal prayer from members of local church house groups. After twelve months ninety per cent of this group were still alive and most of them doing very well, whereas of the other group, who had received no prayer support, only ten per cent were left, many of whom were quite sick. This example of more direct, divine healing takes place where otherwise the patients' welfare would have depended on the ordinary, albeit God-given skill of doctors, indicates very clearly the effectiveness of prayer for healing when combined with normal medical procedures.

The Bible gives a few instances of God ordaining healing through natural methods. Hezekiah was given a fig poultice for his fatal boil (2 Kings 20:7) and Paul advised his student Timothy to take wine for his weak stomach (1 Tim. 5:23). It is very important, however, to make a clear distinction between *indirect* healing of the sort that occurs when you take an aspirin for your headache, and *direct* healing that happens when through the laying on of hands you are rid of a migraine. As Straton wrote, 'God's healing is not on the lower plane of medicine . . . but on the higher plane of the supernatural.' Divine healing is based not on knowledge and science, but on the power that proceeds from Christ's atonement and resurrection. One great benefit of the first is the way it gives us confidence to approach God for the second – something which the second century writer Titan noted when he asked, 'Why is he who trusts in the system of matter, that is, healing by medicine, not willing to trust in God?'

The last enemy

I used to say I'd seen the Lord work every kind of miracle except the raising of the dead. Certainly it was a rare miracle even in biblical times, for although Jesus healed multitudes in the three years of his earthly ministry, he raised up only three – Lazarus, Dorcas and Jairus' daughter. In the case of Lazarus the miracle was effectively set up as a sign of Jesus' power over death and impending resurrection. But if this power was formally passed on to the Apostles they do not seem to have had much incentive to use it; in fact in the rest of the New Testament we find only two more instances of the dead being raised, once by Paul and once by Peter.

But if the raising of the dead is a rare miracle there is ample evidence that it is still happening. In my travels to the Far East I have been given several reliable accounts of the miracle occurring in Indonesia. In Britain the evangelist Smith Wigglesworth successfully raised people from the dead on at least three occasions – in fact while pioneering a church in the early days I met one of them. After dying and being resurrected, he lived for another thirty-nine years, and though he was an old man by the time I saw him he showed no signs of hurrying back to his grave!

None the less until very recently I had never actually witnessed a resurrection, and was foolish enough to say as much at a meeting I held in the West Country. I say I was foolish because the very next night the Lord took me to task about it. We were preaching in the town hall of a small country community, and the worship was going ahead nicely when quite out of the blue a man near the back of the room doubled over off his seat and sprawled on the floor. It was over in a matter of seconds; immediately the stewards gathered round him, but when a nurse came forward a moment later his pulse had already stopped. Before word was passed to me on the platform his heart had stopped too. He was dead.

I prayed quietly. In the circumstances we ought to be sending for an ambulance, though by the time one reached us it would be far too late to resuscitate him: if there was any hope of that it depended on the nurse and the people here, and they were already doing all they could. Another thing weighed on my mind as well. Ambulance or no ambulance, a man dying at a healing crusade would cause a lot of adverse publicity; recriminations and misunderstandings would be rife. And that wasn't going to help God's work in the least. This consideration more than any other moved me to get to my feet and pray: a hush fell on the congregation as I told them what had happened, and explained that we were going to claim God's resurrection power. Then we prayed, hundreds of us, in one mind and with one faith . . .

The meeting continued. I gave a brief sermon and invited people to come forward for salvation, and then began praying for the sick. It was out of the corner of my eye that I saw, at the back, the dead man getting to his feet. He got up, walked around, then sat down again. When he left the meeting at the end he waved. No one, least of all me, would have guessed that his heart had ceased to beat for fifteen minutes – that he had missed the whole of my sermon because he was clinically dead. And yet it could not be denied. The medical facts were verified by a qualified SRN and the minister of the local church. I had seen my first raising of the dead.

That it took me so long to see it serves to emphasise its contrast to ordinary healing. It is God's will and part of his loving care for his people that we should be kept in divine health, and that is why the healing gift has been given to the church. At the same time it is the one certain fact about human life that it will come to an end. Death has been written into the dynamics of the universe from the day of man's fall. In Paul's words, 'The whole creation groaneth and travaileth in pain together until now' (Rom. 8:22). This inevitability of death has engendered all sorts of gloomy reflection in world literature, from Wordsworth's observation that 'shades of the prison house begin to chase upon the growing boy' to the blacker moods of the Preacher: 'Man knoweth not his time: as the fishes are caught in an evil net . . . so are the sons of men snared in an evil time, when it falleth suddenly upon them' (Eccles. 9:12).

It is one of the main arguments of Ecclesiastes that human life is pointless and transient, and this is a sentiment that finds an echo in many hearts today. Why seek healing? Why strive for the good and the right when in the end death will reduce all our efforts to nothing? How we answer this question, of course, depends on how we view death. If death is, as Baroness Wooten urged, 'the extinction of human consciousness' then we have nothing to hope for and little incentive for positive action. But Christian faith opens up another option. Without denying the sadness of bereavement – after all, about to raise Lazarus from the dead Jesus wept before his tomb – we can see death as a changing of trains, and not as a terminus. As the country writer Mary Webb puts it, 'Death is a gate on the skyline.' Since the resurrection of Christ it is impossible for the Christian to see it in any other way. We are simply going on to that land where Jesus is already preparing a place for us, and therefore the brevity of life that so frustrates the humanist and the unbeliever is for us a blessing in disguise, as life itself is only the prelude to something far greater. Thus death, that arch-weapon of the enemy, becomes an instrument of grace.

'Death of deatns, and hell's destruction, lands me safe on Canaan's side.'

Much of what frightens us about death is the pain and confusion that often go with it. And that is why I feel there is a way of dying that is to death what divine healing is to life. In the words of Howard Cobb, 'The God who is the author of life does not need disease to destroy life. When he is ready he can quietly withdraw the life he gave and call his child . . . Such passings are not infrequent . . . they are more in accordance with the will of the Father than the passings brought about by agonising death.' This sort of passing, the kind which comes without distress at the end of a happy, healthy life, is what we should pray for, both for ourselves and for others.

But we must face up to the fact that at least in some cases death is unpleasant, protracted, and untimely despite the best efforts of praying Christians. A notable example of this is David Watson, whose death through cancer I have repeatedly been challenged to explain. After all, here was a valuable Christian minister prayed for by men widely acknowledged to have the gift of healing. As his faith and theirs could hardly have been stronger, it seems like a test case. Why then did David Watson die? Is it proof that in the final analysis there is no real divine healing today?

I am perfectly sure it isn't. No one ever proved a general principle on the basis of a single case, least of all in the matter of healing where there are so many unknown factors at work. My own experience, anyway, contradicts a con-conclusion of that sort, as I have seen many people with conditions similar to David Watson's healed instantly. What I recall about his particular illness is that when it was first made public a prophecy was given to the effect that 'this will fall out to the glory of God.' And this undoubtedly has happened, not least because when David Watson died he was prepared for his death and reconciled to it. 'I believe not just in life after death,' he said, 'but in life through death.' And so it is my opinion that in the higher purposes of God David Watson was asked to teach us all a lesson – how to die even in dreadful circumstances with Christian dignity, with assurance, lofty Christian character and courage. No one who saw him in his last days will ever forget his calmness, his confidence, his graciousness. He showed that Spirit-filled Christians know how to die well.

And whether we live long and healthy lives or, as is sometimes God's calling, go to be with the Lord at an earlier stage, we will all have to face the fact that our departure from his life is the only way of attaining the next. But the victory does not belong to death; Jesus robbed it of that long ago. In Bunyan's *Pilgrim's Progress* Christian finally descended into the swirling waters crying, 'Death, where is thy sting?' and 'Death, where is thy victory?' And so the trumpets played for him as he passed over to the other side.

There will come a time when death is swallowed up in victory and forgotten. 'God shall wipe away all tears from their eyes; and there shall be no more death, neither sorrow, nor crying, neither shall there be any more pain . . . ' (Rev. 21.4). The removal of death is part of the healing of the nations that God will undertake in the last time, that greater healing of which the present gift is a mere shadow. When every trace of evil has been eliminated from God's new heaven and new earth, 'The last enemy that shall be destroyed is death' (1 Cor. 15:26).

9: Miracle at the Bull

He ministereth to you the Spirit, and worketh miracles among you.

St Paul

Mr. Bollard picked up the telephone and dialled the number on the crumpled leaflet in his lap. There was a crackle as the line connected.

'Hello?'

'Hello, is that the miracle service?'

A dull thud told him a hand had been placed over the mouthpiece at the other end. He heard faintly a child's voice say, 'Daddy, it's someone wanting to know about the miracles.' Bollard glanced at his wife who was sitting in her wheelchair, knitting. They looked at each other, but neither of them spoke.

'Pastor Mawes speaking,' the line crackled.

'Yes, good evening, Mr Mawes. I'm phoning about the service.'

'Yes.'

'It's still on, isn't it?'

'Yes, indeed. Are you coming along tonight?'

'I want to bring my wife. She's been in a chair these last couple of years, you see, and we had your leaflet put through our door this morning.'

'Where are you phoning from?'

'From Swindon.'

'You're not too far away, then. I must tell you there's been a last minute change of venue. One of the churches supporting us pulled out yesterday and we can't use the hall that's printed on the advertisements.'

'So where should we go?'

'To the Bull.'

Mr Bollard's pen, which had been poised to write on the back of the leaflet, drew a short indecisive line.

'Where did you say?'

'The Bull Hotel. If you come up the Gloucester Road you can't miss it. It's right on the crossroads opposite the post office.

Mr Bollard mouthed at his wife, 'It's happening in a pub!'

'Are you still there?'

'Yes, I was just saying . . . I mean – you're saying the miracle service is going to be in a public house?'

'Yes.'

The voice, pulled thin by the telephone, sounded on the verge of laughter.

'Are you allowed to take church services in a pub?'

'The proprietor didn't mind. And you know in the Gospels Jesus was always mixing with publicans and sinners . . .'

But Mr Bollard didn't get the joke.

'Right, well, thank you very much, and we'll see you tonight. Seven o'clock?'

'Seven o'clock. Bye.'

Mr Bollard replaced the receiver with the sort of grin he got after winning a game of billards. 'Well, love a duck,' he said.

They arrived at the Bull at a quarter past seven to find a queue outside the front door. It was the first time Mr Bollard had had to queue to get into a pub since the Coronation. A woman steward – the barmaid? – was stooping down at the bottom. 'Next service 8.15,' she wrote. 'Please leave after first service to make room for others.' Mr Bollard stepped forward.

'Are we too late?'

'I'm afraid you'll have to wait for the next service.'

'But I have my wife out here in the cold . . . .'

'There just isn't any room.'

'Can't you squeeze us in somewhere?'

The woman stood up and reluctantly pushed the door open. It led into a small porch with frosted glass windows. A sign on their right said *Men only*; the steward went left through the public bar to the green baize door of a conference room. When she pushed it gave just far enough for Mr Bollard to see a crowd of heads and a piano. Someone poked his head around.

'Any room?'

'You'll be lucky.'

'We have a lady can't wait in the cold.'

'Well, if she can get in, I'll give her my seat.'

The steward glanced back at Mr Bollard.

'Actually, she's in a wheelchair . . . ' he said.

'Oh, no!'

'Don't you think it might be better to wait . . . ?' the steward said weakly.

But Mr Bollard wasn't going back now. 'Can't you get that door open any further?' he said. The man inside stood up and began shooing people away from the door, and in half a minute Mr Bollard could see, to the left of the piano, a table with a vase of chrysanthemums. 'This woman had been sick for twelve years,' said a voice. 'She'd gone to the doctors and they'd done nothing for her. She'd spent all her money. No National Health Service in those days. She was at the end of the road . . . '

'All right, dear,' Mr Bollard said, steering his wife's chair over the step and into the porch. He noticed this time a yellow poster on the bar door with a smudged photograph of someone called Melvin Banks. 'Coming to Swannington Church Hall,' it said.

'Can you imagine what it was like for her, trying to reach Jesus in that crowd? Have you ever tried walking through a football crowd to get to the other end of the stand? By the time you're half way over you can't see where you're going any more, can you? That's what it was like for that woman. She was one person, one sick person, in a whole mass of men and women who were trying to get close to Jesus. You know, if it had been you or I, we might well have given up before we reached him . . . '

'Sorry,' said Mr Bollard.

One of the footpads on his wife's wheelchair had just rapped someone's ankle. The lady scowled at him, but now he was into the room he had little alternative but to go on. He looked apologetically at the speaker. For some reason the man bore a striking resemblance to the photograph on the door. It was only when Melvin Banks grinned at him that Mr Bollard made the connection.

'I think you'd better come right through to the front.'

Mr Bollard squeezed on to the end of a bench by his wife and mopped his brow. He hadn't seen so many people crammed into a bar since Bristol Rovers were promoted, and no one here was wearing a scarf or a woolly cap. None of them were drinking, either.

'She knew,' went on Melvin Banks, 'that she only needed to touch the hem of his garment. She didn't need a long prayer. She didn't really want to be noticed . . . '

Nor did I, thought Mr Bollard.

'But she had the sort of faith that made her get through that big crowd and do that very little thing – to touch the hem of Jesus' cloak. Like this . . .,' Melvin Banks tweaked the lapel of his blazer. 'Just a touch, and she would be healed. Do you believe that? Do you believe you only need the touch of Jesus to make you well? It's true. And if you want, here, tonight, in the Bull Hotel, you can receive that touch . . . '

Mr and Mrs Bollard listened. At the end of the sermon they prayed the sinners' prayer and filled in a counselling card. They joined in the songs, and then they watched as the speaker laid his hands on a woman with arthritis. She laid down her sticks, she stood up, she walked, she jumped. 'Love a duck,' whispered Mr Bollard to his wife.

The miracles came one after another. A deaf woman began to hear, a little child who had a stutter started to say long sentences over clearly while his mother wept beside him. Then Melvin Banks came over to Mrs Bollard.

'Let's get these foot treads up.'

'It hurts.'

'I know. Are you ready to walk?'

'I don't know if I can . . . '

'Don't worry about that. Just let your feet touch the ground so you're ready to go. You let nothing stop you getting in here. Now there's nothing to stop you walking out.'

He prayed, and Mrs Bollard felt the pain vanish and a new energy press into her feet.

'It's lovely,' she said. 'I can feel my feet!'

'Now get up and walk . . . '

In the small space at the front of the room Mrs Bollard rose to her feet and began to walk. The crowd cleared in front of her, and she walked all the way to the door; then she walked through the door and out into the street where the queue now stretched half way round the building. Everyone began to clap. Mr Bollard, who had been looking at her in amazement, suddenly unfolded the wheelchair and wheeled it out after her – the last time in fact, that it was used, because Mrs Bollard has been healthy and mobile ever since.

When at another meeting she returned to give her testimony, she was introduced as the Miracle of the Bull Hotel.

Importunity pays

That is the message of Mr and Mrs Bollard's story. Importunity pays. It is not sitting on our backsides and making idle wishes that gets us what we seek. It never has been, in any sphere of life. It is the men and women who know what they want, who stick by their guns, who are in the end rewarded and achieve great things. Christopher Columbus had to trek round the courts of Spain pleading for financial support before he could rig out his ships and discover the New World. Winston Churchill used to say in the darkest hours of the Second World War, 'Never give up, never give up' – and because he never did give up the Allies won.

It is noticeable that in the Gospel records the sick individuals who sought out the Saviour were always healed.

The blind man who cried out, 'Son of David, have mercy on me!' when his friends were telling him to shut up and be quiet was called out from the crowd and given his sight (Luke 18:38). He had faith; he knew that the source of his healing, the Word of God, was passing by; he knew that the opportunity for his release of faith had come. All the same he could have kept quiet and stopped making a fool of himself–he had only his faith to go on, and everyone thought he was crazy shouting to Jesus. But he had importunity, and his importunity paid. It got him to the place where his faith could produce healing. It made his faith work.

Importunity also involves *persistence*. At the beginning of the same chapter in which the blind man is healed we read that Jesus 'spake a parable unto them to this end, that men ought always to pray, and not to faint . . . ' (Luke 18:1). The parable is about a judge and a widow. The judge is a mean character who sells justice for bribes. The widow is seeking vindication against her adversary in the court of law. The judge would not normally be predisposed to favour her – she is poor, and so her rights don't feature highly on his list of urgent business. But the woman is persistent; in fact she's a wretched nuisance. Every day he gets letters and visits, and in the end he decides to grant her request because she'll drive him nuts if he doesn't. 'And shall not God avenge his own elect,' says Jesus, 'which cry day and night unto him, though he bear long with them? I tell you, he will average them speedily' (Luke 18:7, 8).

God honours those who go out of their way to seek him, and persist even when he seems not to be listening. If an unjust judge, who usually responds only to bribes, gives his judgment as a result of persistent badgering, how much more true will it be of God, who is ready and willing to give good gifts to his children. We must be importunate in prayer. We must keep asking and pleading. Kenneth Hagin once said, 'If the anointing wanes in my life, I do a little extra praying and more fasting, and it comes back in force!' It is true. I have found it to be the case myself in seeking God's power for the healing ministry. And if we keep on seeking and requesting and petitioning and believing, we will receive all things.

But importunity is sometimes hard to keep up. It is like swimming against a current everyone else is drifting along with. We may feel like Timorous, who told Christian in Bunyan's *Pilgrim's Progress* that 'The farther we go the more danger and evil we meet with; wherefore we turned and are going back again . . . ' Timorous had given up and let himself be swept back with the tide of evil. Life was too much for him to cope with. And life can hit any of us pretty hard. When Paul writes to the Romans, 'Be not overcome of evil,' he is not making an abstract statement. The Greek word translated 'evil' is *kakos*, which in this context means a particular evil personally inflicted, a wrong suffered at the hands of an enemy. The same word is used in the letter to Timothy when Paul says, 'Alexander the Coppersmith did me much evil' (2 Tim. 4:14).

But there is more. To 'Be not overcome of evil' Paul adds 'but overcome evil with good' (Rom 12.21). He could have used three Greek words for good: he could have used *dikaios*, which refers to pure, rather clinical righteousness, or *kalos*, meaning good in outward appearance, or beautiful. But he used neither of these terms. What Paul was talking about was robust, through and through moral goodness – what the Greeks called *agathos*. The good tree producing good fruit was *agathos*; so too was the good ground which brought forth a hundredfold, and the good and faithful servant who in the parable of the talents returned a rich investment to his master. Thus Paul gives us two pictures of the Christian's fight with evil. He can be overcome by it, as one wrestler is overcome and pinned down by another. Or he can overcome it, surround and submerge it with goodness. The true sense of the original verse is 'Be not conquered *under evil*, but conquer evil *in the good*.' Evil can be subjugated under the pressure of goodness as we let the Holy Spirit work in us for our sanctification. In this battle it is not upright, technical goodness we require – that state of sinlessness before God that even the best of us can never achieve – it is the inward healthy goodness that comes from the simple fact of our faith in God. Something given, not something we have to aim for. The good tree in Jesus' parable didn't sit around waiting until it was good enough to produce fruit – it just went ahead and grew, and fruit came naturally because it was a good tree. The storms and wind and rain made no difference to it. It shrugged them off because it already had the inner strength to hold up and keep going.

So it is with the attacks of evil that come to us. We may be discouraged, we may have unkind things said to us, we may feel too tired to persist in prayer. But we can overcome the evil with the good that is already in us. We don't lie down and take the punishment; we move forward in the same confidence Wellington had in the furore of Waterloo: 'Hard pounding this, gentlemen. Let us see who will pound the longest.' It is when we keep pounding, keep pushing, keep persistent, that we conquer. If Norman Vincent Peale could make people believe in themselves through the power of positive thinking, how much more confidence can we have in the strength of God's goodness. In his power, 'make yourself believe you are a better and more competent person than you ever thought you were . . . that you are unconquerable.'

To finish, I want to give two more examples of this kind of importunity.

A few years ago I received a request to hold a crusade meeting in a small country town. It came from six elderly ladies. I wrote what I thought to be a polite and sensible refusal, explaining that the team didn't *usually* work in pioneer situations without at least ten local helpers or the support of a group of churches. It didn't deter them; a few days later they replied that the Lord had told them I was going to come. But didn't they realise, I wrote again, that a crusade would mean putting up scores of posters and delivering about sixteen thousand leaflets? Yes, they did. And what's more they were going to do the whole lot themselves. In the end I stayed in the town for six nights, and God honoured the importunity of these six old ladies with a full hall every night, several outstanding miracles, and three hundred converts!

More recently I was honoured to visit a man called Sim Beck Whee in a remote part of the Malaysian rain forest. He had been pestering the minister at the Assemblies of God Church in Malacca – the Rev Robert Suppiah – to let me break my schedule and drive the fifty miles out of Malacca to pray for his daughter, who was paralysed from the waist down and too ill to be driven in for the crusade. Robert Suppiah's excuses on my behalf went unheeded, and in the end he agreed to let me go, though he knew I was dog tired and still had several big meetings to take before the tour ended. We set off in a van into the recesses of the jungle . . .

Mr Sim Beck Whee tells the story in his own words:

'Shortly after moving to this area from northern Malaysia my eldest daughter Lee Gaik became paralysed. It happened for no apparent reason. I sent her to a child specialist who confirmed that Lee Gaik was suffering with a rare virus infection which attacks the spinal cord and nervous system. She eventually lost her voice and could not even gather enough strength to drink, due to the weak muscle movement in her throat. There was even a danger she might suffocate.

This was all like a bombshell to us. It was unbearable. I became very sorrowful and a little bitter at our misfortune. I began to pray with some Christian friends, but she only got worse. One day, as she was growing very sick, I read an advertisement in the newspaper that an evangelist from England was coming to conduct a crusade in the Malacca Town Hall. I had a strange feeling this was the answer to our grave dilemma. I called the minister whose number was on the advertisement, explained how sick my child was, and he agreed to bring Rev Banks to my home to pray for her.

What a wonderful day when the evangelist arrived, that God should send him all the way from the UK to minister to my hopeless child. He came into the house and declared that the idols must be burned, and I agreed to do this. He then prayed and exorcised the house. He laid hands on my daughter and straight away as he used the name of Jesus again and again she seemed to be revived. He prayed for about ten minutes and he was sweating as he earnestly called upon God. To my utter amazement, her critical, hopeless and lifeless condition began to change, and within two days she became normal!

Since then she has never been fitter. She is even top of her class in one subject. When I sent her back to the specialist he could only say 'Wonderful, wonderful, marvellous!' He was overwhelmed by her health and wanted to know how it was done. We told him God had done it all. This great miracle has spread far and wide. We have gone through the hard way, and have been through a lot of difficulties, but God brought us through. We have tasted and seen that the Lord is good.'

The moral: *It pays to be persistent!*

10: How Not to be Healed

Man has conquered everything . . . he has only to conquer his last and worst enemy – himself.

Winston Churchill

Human beings are very fond of complaining. It generates a sort of warmth. Two holiday-makers sitting resolutely in their deckchairs on a bleak Blackpool beach will roll their eyes and say, 'Bloomin' awful summer we're 'avin',' and immediately they feel a little better. After an eight-nil trouncing at the cup final they will agree it would all have been different if the ref hadn't awarded that penalty in the first three minutes; and when the price of beer goes up by two pence a pint they'll call it daylight robbery and cheer each other up by moaning over the rate of inflation. We're all the same. If the universe is treating us badly there's nothing better than sitting down and telling someone about it. It's unjust, it should have happened to someone else, and something really ought to be done about it, we always say. Which leads us on to another popular pastime – the *Blame Game*. Nothing hard about this; you just choose your favourite complaint and then malign the person you feel is most to be held responsible for it. Chief objects of malice are: the government or 'the people in charge of things' (often referred to as *they* or *them*), the wife or husband, your employer (or employees), and sometimes – for want of anything more definite – God.

Scoring in the *Blame Game* is a matter of some subtlety, because it depends on inferring that, put in the shoes of the person you're accusing, you'd have done a better job than they did. This requires careful scrutiny of your opponent. If he or she knows a bit about, say, economics, you might find yourself in trouble with the blunt assertion that 'The government is to blame for unemployment.' No doubt the government should shoulder some of the blame; but your opponent may point out that any government is subject to certain unavoidable pressures and that unemployment also has to do with longer-term changes like automation and the decline of manufacturing industry. So what would you have done in the same circumstances?

This may not be a very good example, but it introduces us to the fact that no situation in life is terribly straightforward. When things go wrong there may not be a single factor of which I can say: 'There, that's what's causing the trouble.' It may be many things together. It may even – something a Blame-Gamer is loath to admit – be me myself. Nowhere is this more true than in healing. It cannot be said for certain what proportion of people prayed for actually receive what we might call a significant measure of healing; because more and more healings occur in my meetings without any formal laying on of hands, a lot slip through the statistical net. Where healing cards have been filled in and cases followed up by local church congregations the figure appears to be around two thirds, which leaves a thirty per cent failure rate – those who, for some reason or other, have not been healed.

A common explanation for failure put forward by those in the healing ministry is that the person prayed for lacked faith. It may be true. But I personally would never use that as an excuse – as far as I am concerned it is a matter of principle that if a person is not healed I am the one at fault. Not the sick man or woman. Not the church where I am ministering. Me. 'But if it is God who does the healing,' a television interviewer once asked, 'surely you cannot be held responsible for the failures?' The answer is that I can: no human being is infallible, and just as we all find relief in complaining and blaming others so are we all blameworthy. In fact it is often our own sense of guilt that makes us want to prove everyone else is guilty too.

But of course I am speaking from my own perspective here. If I have prayed for you and you have not been healed, it may be that the 'blockage' lies in you and not in me. In a way that is none of my business and it is rather rude of me to suggest it; but it will help things along if you have a look at your weaknesses while I'm having a look at mine. If you blame me for not praying properly, and I blame you for not having faith, then neither of us will get any further! My only advantage at this point is that praying for around forty thousand people every year I have come to see what sort of problems prevent someone getting healed, so I summarise them here simply as a piece of friendly advice. I call them the Ten Commandments of healing, though really they're more like a checklist of faults. If the light goes out in your living room you don't immediately panic and phone the electricity board – you try out one or two simple tests. First, change the bulb; if that fails, check the fuses; if they're okay, look down the street to see if everyone else's lights are out as well . . . and so on. So here are ten possible failure-points which must be cleared if the healing 'light' is going to shine as it should.

(1) Look at Jesus, not the person praying.
When Peter healed the lame man at Jerusalem's Beautiful Gate, a great crowd gathered to ogle at him. But Peter only said, 'Ye men of Israel, why marvel ye at this; or why look ye so earnestly on us, as though by our own power or holiness we had made this man to walk?' (Acts. 3:12). It wasn't Peter who had healed, but God – and yet the crowd's first reaction was to think the miracle had come from Peter. This happens all the time. Perhaps for that reason God chooses as his servants those who would not naturally be regarded as great or heroic. Moses, used by God to bring his people out of Egypt and lead them through the wilderness, seems to have had a speech impediment; and Gideon, called upon to lead Israel against the Midianites, could hardly believe God's call because he was the least important member of the least important tribe. 'But we have this treasure in earthen vessels,' wrote Paul of the Spirit's gifts, 'that the excellency of the power may be of God and not of us' (2 Cor. 4:7). The minister is nothing, his God everything; and to mistake one for the other is essentially idolatrous – making a god of

someone or something that is only a creature of God. The Lord sometimes makes this clear by healing through Christians who do not have the reputation of a healing ministry. One person I know of travelled thousands of miles to be prayed for by a special evangelist, and was later healed by the prayers of his local congregation! The Bible does not say that famous evangelists are the *only* people we can go to for healing; indeed, when James recommends the sick to seek God's healing touch he has in mind the local church elders.

(2) Don't be half-hearted.
'Ye shall seek me and find me when ye shall search for me with all your heart,' said the Lord through his prophet Jeremiah (Jer. 29:13). God wants to know that we're serious and persistent in our requests. If like me you have children, you will be used to acting as PR man for Santa Claus. You will also have taken an order for some impossibly expensive toy that you suspect your child will never use, and probably you argued the toss about whether he really wanted it. After all, he'd never mentioned it before! A person who really wants something wants it enough to nag. And often they'll keep on nagging till they get it. Elijah on Mount Carmel got down on his knees and prayed for rain until he had to put up his umbrella. He didn't give up at the first attempt because the sky remained imperturbably blue. He prayed in earnest, in desperation. And that is how we are to pray for healing. We must keep on battering the door as though we can do no more until it opens for us. Nor must we turn back in discouragement; as General Orde Wingate said to his British guerrillas in Burma during the last war, 'Don't report any jungle inpenetrable until it has been penetrated!'

(3) Be prepared.
When the Sadducees came to cavil with Jesus on their favourite controversy – whether or not there was such a miracle as resurrection – he replied, 'Ye do err, not knowing the scriptures, nor the power of God' (Matt. 22:29). Many

receive healing at my meetings knowing the power of God, but not knowing the Scriptures. That is as it should be. But at the same time your openness to healing is greatly increased by spreading the word. Jesus spent most of his time on earth teaching the word of God, and teaching is reckoned above the working of miracles in Paul's list of Christian ministries in the first Epistle to the Corinthians (1 Cor. 12:28). Sound faith is built upon sound teaching, and sound faith is of great benefit in receiving healing. It is thus an important exercise in preparation for healing to soak yourself in the word of God.

(4) Don't limit God to instant miracles.
It is easy in an age of instant coffee and instant mashed potatoes to think a miracle is defective unless it happens right away. There is no scriptural support for this. Many miracles were instant, but several were not. A blind man prayed over by Jesus first of all saw men as vague shapes like trees (Mark 8:24). The faithful nobleman was told when he returned from his encounter with the Saviour that his sick servant had been healed; yet at the moment of prayer he had not instantly leapt up from his bed, but 'begun to amend' (John 4:52). Similarly, ten lepers are said to have received their healing as they made their way to the priests – a description indicating that healing here was gradual and not instantaneous (Luke 17:14). The same has been true of my own ministry. Some have been healed in their cars on the way home from a meeting and some after an interval of weeks or months. Some, like the nobleman's servant, begin to amend when hands are laid on them. These healings are no less special than the instant ones, in fact it is often the case that the Spirit is doing some greater work in a man's soul as his body is gradually healed. So do not be discouraged if healing is slow or delayed.

(5) Take a look at your motives.
This may sound a bit funny – after all, the motive for seeking

healing is surely to be healed. But ask yourself what you would do if you *were* healed. Might you not plunge straight back into the life you led before, and forget God? If so, you are really coming to God with conditions, trying to strike a deal with him on entirely your own terms. But there are no JRs in heaven; there isn't, strictly speaking, any business of the sort we would recognise. The economics of God's Kingdom tend to be based on giving things away free, and God is the biggest spiritual millionaire because he's given more away more completely than anybody else. If he doesn't exactly make our giving something back to him a condition of our healing then it is certainly true that receiving healing draws us into giving ourselves to God, and a determination to hang on to our assets makes any kind of 'deal' impossible. 'Forgive us our trespasses as we forgive those who trespass against us.' It's all a bit like falling in love. It won't happen unless you are willing to give love as well as receive it, but when you start giving you find that giving actually helps you to receive, and the more you give the better everything becomes. Also, if you are a man, you will know that the woman who gives her love freely in exchange for yours is very different from the one who gives love – of a limited sort – in exchange for money. By this analogy, God is a lover and not a prostitute.

(6) Let go your self-pity.
The sick sometimes develop a *sickness complex*, and use their sickness as a lever to manipulate others into giving them sympathy. They want everyone to know just how much they're suffering. The problem is that they get to rely on it and cannot imagine how to relate to others without this manipulative device, with the result that sickness becomes a prop every bit as necessary to them in psychological terms as a walking stick is to a man who is lame. The response made by Peter to Jesus' prediction of his death (Matt. 16:22) is translated in the Revised Version, 'Pity thyself', and it is a measure of how destructive this kind of sentiment can be that Jesus rebuked his friend in the strongest possible terms:

'Get thee behind me, Satan: thou art an offence unto me . . .' Self-pity is a subtle form of selfishness, and if we are to find healing it must be renounced.

(7) Kick out your sins.

The Bible is perfectly blunt about sin. 'If I regard iniquity in my heart,' wrote the psalmist, 'the Lord will not hear me' (Ps. 66:18). There is a difference between sinning and regarding iniquity. All of us sin right up to our dying day whether we are Christians or not; what makes the believer distinctive is that he has, in his heart, turned against sin. He doesn't regard it, cherish it, or pay homage to it: as soon as he recognises something as a sin he boots it out. If he doesn't, then he is turning against God. As Jesus said, no one can serve two masters without preferring one over the other, and it stands to reason that God will not hear us if we insist on serving another master besides him. 'Your sins have hid his face from you,' Isaiah tells the wicked (Isa. 59:2). Sin deafens God's ears to our prayers and undermines the faith in which we present them; which is why we are urged in Scripture to examine our consciences continually and to help our fellow believers (though with great tact) to examine theirs. Paul advises Timothy that he should be 'in meekness instructing those that oppose themselves; if God peradventure will give them repentance to the acknowledging of the truth' (2 Tim. 2:25). Repentance and confession clear the decks and open the way for healing. And that may take some careful thought and prayer, for many of the most obstructive sins – like unforgiveness, bitterness and resentment – are hardest to see, and when seen only grudgingly acknowledged to be sins. None the less God will if we ask him lead us to identify those sins that are holding up our healing and give us strength to reject them.

(8) Don't be hard-hearted.

One of the most fabulous displays of hard-heartedness in the Bible comes in the book of Genesis, where Joseph's brothers, having just thrown him into a pit, sit down for a picnic (Gen. 37:25). A hard heart is one that is so obsessed with its own purposes that it ignores the welfare of others. It sits with its boots up on the verandah watching men slave for fourteen hours on a sugar plantation; it switches over to another channel when an appeal for famine aid comes on the television; it idles around while a healing goes on and calls it disgraceful because Sunday is a day of rest. This sort of hard-heartedness, typical of the pharisees at the time of Jesus, is most like the sort we encounter in healing. The hard-hearted person will refuse to admit there's any good in it, and instead of welcoming healing he looks for things to criticise. 'These healing meetings create a disturbance at night,' he will say, or, 'It usually does more harm than good; your illness might get a bit better, but look what a crowd you're getting yourself into . . . ' That kind of attitude is only set right by humility, for it is when we humble ourselves under the mighty hand of God that he will exalt us in healing.

(9) Leave unbelief.

Unbelief, the habit of not trusting and not expecting, is a major barrier to healing. Everyone can be healed who wants to be healed, but we must all meet God's conditions, and these begin with *faith*. Jesus, healing the blind man, said, 'According to your faith be if unto you' (Matt. 9:29). Their eyes were opened because they believed. Suppose they'd said, 'Well, really we're not quite sure you can do this. We'll give it a try, but you must understand that, just in case it fails, we're not building up our hopes too far . . . ' If they'd said that, they'd have been blind for the rest of their lives. At some point you have to commit yourself, as a little girl jumping from a fence commits herself in the faith that her father will catch her. Doubt has only one consolation: that of being able to say, 'I told you so.' And its predictions are correct because, as Norman Vincent Peale points out, 'By not being positive, we create those actual conditions that lead to failure.' So take no notice of unbelieving friends, unbelieving Christians, unbelieving ministers. Ditch your unbelief and have faith.

(10) Forgive

A woman I saw on the news recently said of a wrong that had been done to her that she would forgive, but would never forget. Admittedly her suffering was greater than anything I have ever had to face, and all traumatic experiences leave an indelible imprint on the memory. But that wasn't, I think, what she meant by never forgetting. She was really not forgiving at all, only suppressing her resentment and hatred to a point where they were more or less invisible to others. I am not criticising her, for who knows how any of us would react in similar circumstances. Nevertheless, Spurgeon's advice is well taken: 'Forgive and forget; when you bury a mad dog, do not leave his tail above the ground!' I suspect that many of us have some tails sticking up in our back gardens: hurtful remarks we've never shaken off, an injustice done and never apologised for, perhaps a simple misunderstanding. And the fact is that until we are willing to forgive others, we cannot be fully forgiven ourselves. Once again, 'Forgive us our trespasses as we forgive those that trespass against us.' Jesus was firm that we can approach God on the single basis of our reconciliation to others, whether we have wronged them or, being wronged, have not forgiven – '. . . first be reconciled to thy brother, and then come and offer thy gift' (Matt. 5:24). This is hard to take: it disqualifies us from the *Blame Game*. It may require us to forgive someone we have never met, who is completely unrepentant, who may still bear us malice – and to forgive him so entirely that the very moment we find ourselves harbouring evil thoughts about him we realise we are in the wrong and owe him an apology. Pretty tough talk – but it comes from Jesus himself, whose steps we are pledged to follow even to the cross, where the greatest injustice of all was committed. 'Then said Jesus, "Father, forgive them; for they know not what they do"' (Luke 23:34). Yet if getting rid of bitterness is harder than uprooting a dead oak tree, it can always be done in God's strength; and when it is gone, the way may be clear for our healing.

11: The Silences of God

Light your lamp before it is dark.

Harold Coleman

When David Watson lay dying of cancer he received from the Bishop of Southwark a letter which included this statement: 'The greatest test of the Christian life is to live with the silences of God.' That God should be silent at the times when we are weak and needy is almost inconceivable. Didn't Jesus promise that he would be with his people even to the end of the earth? (Matt. 28:20). Yet sometimes our experience is precisely that.

One of the most telling moments in Francis Ford Copolla's film *Apocalypse Now* comes when an officer arrives on the scene of an ambush. All around him lie the bodies of American sevicemen. The ones who have survived the massacre are horribly wounded and it is only their groans that break an eerie silence. The officer goes from soldier to soldier demanding 'Who's in charge here?' It is a ridiculous and pathetic question, but it finds an echo in all human response to suffering because with every natural disaster, every fatal accident, every illness, someone will shake his fist and cry at the empty heavens, 'Who's in charge here? Who let this outrage happen?' Even Christians, who for years have served the Lord they know to be in command of the universe, may when the trial comes upon them ask whether they have not been abandoned. It is the way of the cross: 'And at about the ninth hour Jesus cried with a loud voice, saying, "Eli, Eli, lama sabachthani?" that is to say, "My God, my God, why hast thou forsaken me?"' (Matt. 27:46).

Life brings everyone their little crucifixions; times when

prayers bounce back, when there is no comfort, no feeling of warmth or reassurance, no still small voice. 'The speechlessness of God,' said the playwright Tennessee Williams, 'is a long, long terrible thing.' The Bible gives him plenty of support, for believers of all ages have passed through this valley of the shadow and their reactions are faithfully recorded in the words of the Scripture. Job, the hardest done-by of them all, complained that besides his other trials he had been made to endure the awful absence of God: 'Behold, I go forward, but he is not there; and backward, but I cannot perceive him: on the left hand, where he doth work, but I cannot behold him: he hideth himself on the right hand that I cannot see him' (Job 23:8, 9). To judge by the reproaches of the psalmist, this experience must have been very common. 'I am weary of my crying: my throat is dried: mine eyes fail while I wait for my God' (Ps. 69:3). 'Verily,' concluded Isaiah, 'thou art a God that hidest thyself' (Isa. 45:15).

All this would be incidental if there were easy answers on hand to make the feelings of alienation go away. But that isn't the way it works. I recently ministered to a lady who had long been seeking God's healing touch. 'I have asked and prayed, Mr Banks,' she said. 'I have sought God for my illness. But I hear no voice; I have no assurance, no answer . . . ' I began thumbing through my Bible for a suitable passage – and then realised she must have been through the same procedure countless times already. When I looked up there were tears in her eyes. 'What do you do with failures like me, Mr Banks? What can you do when God is silent?' There is no evading the question; almost all of us are forced to ask it at some time or other, and it had to be honestly and squarely dealt with. What do you do when with the greatest strength you can muster you examine your conscience and your faith and still God and his healing power seem so remote they might as well not exist?

I believe this is one of the most important issues a Christian can ever face. It belongs to the heart of the cross, the very depth of Christ's passion which we his followers are called to emulate. It is something that divides the giants of faith from the babes, and must be taken into our own lives if we are to reach a full maturity. So how do we begin to understand it? After my first encounter with that lady I gave myself to prayer, and felt the Lord directing me to study the seventh chapter of Mark. Things started to fall into place.

Visiting Tyre, we are told, Jesus 'entered into an house, and would have no man know it . . . ' (Mark 7:24). He deliberately hid himself away, made himself inaccessible. 'But he could not be hid, for a certain woman, whose young daughter had an unclean spirit, heard of him, and came and fell at his feet' (vv. 24, 25). I realised that this Syrophenician woman was encountering the silence of God, amazingly, in God's own Word, for not only did Jesus slip unseen into the house, but when she came to seek him out he met her with a pretty blunt rebuff: 'Let the children first be filled, for it is not meet to take the children's bread, and to cast it unto the dogs' (v. 27). How was it then that she finally broke through that silence and received what she so desperately wanted?

For her God's silence could have found its origin in three things. First, this woman carried a *spiritual responsibility*. The order of a household is important in Scripture; God is the head of the man, man the head of the wife, and the wife – as here, in the apparent absence of a husband – is responsible for the children. The fact that her daughter had an unclean spirit was her responsibility. This had to be faced up to before she could appropriate the victory of Jesus over the forces of the Evil One in her daughter. So it is with us. Today we are no less affected by dark spiritual forces than the people of the first century AD, and in approaching God we have to ask ourselves whether through slackness, fickleness or disobedience we have invited Satan into our lives. In such cases the solution to God's 'silence' lies within ourselves.

The second thing we should notice about this woman is that she was *caught up with grief*. We sometimes say we can't see the wood for the trees, meaning that we are too close to something to make out what it really is. This is especially true of emotional problems; they are so overwhelming that under their influence we can see very little else. I have met people in this situation countless times. I recognise them because when I'm counselling them I can hardly get a word in edgeways; they are all over the world with their problem – they're married to it, they live with it, they eat and think it and will eventually drown in it, like the man whose pessimism about life was so profound that when he died his friends (those that he had left, anyway) wrote on his gravestone, *I told you so!* This obsessive attitude to a problem will obscure God just as you can obscure your whole field of vision by standing with your nose against a lamp post. You need to withdraw to get a perspective, and see your difficulty in the context of the life God has given to you. If you do this then what was perceived as the silence of God may turn out to be simple inattention – the way you sometimes fail to hear someone talking to you because you're glued to the TV set.

Third, this woman was an *outsider*. Being a Greek she not only lived outside the commonwealth of Israel, she was also a worshipper of idols, those graven images preserved to us in museums and so explicitly condemned in the Old Testament Law Jesus came to fulfil. When he said, 'Let the children first be fed,' he was talking about God's children, the children of faith, who were the rightful heirs of all the promised blessings (cf. Rom. 9:8). And there is a sense in which all of us are outsiders – if not through our background as Gentiles then because, except for the grace in which we are saved, we are sinful and idolatrous and have no claims on God's mercy. That is why our approach to God is always to be made in humble thanksgiving. At the same time we must remember that the believer has been taken in through the gates of the Kingdom and adopted into God's family, for, as Paul says, 'Ye are all the children of God by faith in Christ Jesus' (Gal. 3:26). The Syrophenician woman was not a child of Israel, yet she attached herself to the family by casting herself on God's mercy. She said, in effect, 'I know I do not belong to your family, Jesus, and I know that your first responsibility is to the children of faith. But if I can claim no higher status than that of the famiily's god, it is still my right to take the leftovers . . . ' Now if this woman asserted her right, as it were on the very fringes of the Kingdom, how much more – to use Paul's phrase – may we children of the promise assert our rights to the promise of God? And how important it is to keep on seeking in the humble knowledge of our past and yet in the confident assurance of our future, towards the promise of God's blessings, even though for a while we cannot sense God near us. In God's silence we may be passing through a mist, ?but our feet stand on the rock.

So this story of the Syrophenician woman suggests three causes of silence in the Almighty: one, some slip which had given Satan a chance to throw us off course, (needing repentance and prayer); two, an obsessive attitude to problems (needing a distancing and a letting-go); and three, a time of dryness in our spiritual experience (through which we need persevering faith). All three are important avenues to explore when we experience the silence of God, though it has to be said that we're on the wrong track if we think we will find any neat, pre-packaged explanations, especially for the third kind. This silence of God is in many ways a mysterious thing, and we may not be able to understand it adequately until we reach the next world. As Howell Harris used to say, if we knew everything, we would be God.

Facing silence

What we can do is make sure we take the right attitude to this silence. Go back again to the story of the Syrophenician woman: she could easily have taken Christ's rebuff as a snub, and walked right out of the house. But she didn't – and that helps us to see that in his silence God is *for* us and not against us. No news, you might say, is good news. In my own prayer life I usually get firm answers to my requests; very often God says yes when I pray for something, and on the occasions when he says no I see later on that it was with a higher purpose in mind, just as it was when Paul, 'forbidden of the Holy Ghost to preach the word in Asia' (Acts 16:6), went on to Philippi to found the church so highly praised in his later epistle. There have been times, however, when God has remained serenely silent when I was almost desperate for reassurance. At Bible college I was unlucky enough to be lambasted by a young faculty member for my rather slow country ways: 'Banks,' he declared, 'you will never make anything!' I was mortified; but although I was driven to prayer to reaffirm my calling, God gave me no answer at all. It was up to me to gird up my own loins and finish what I had determined to begin! And looking back on it I know that God's silence was not a silence of disapproval, but one of love. He wanted me only to have faith and carry on.

Implicit in this acceptance is humility. This is a careful appreciation of one's true position before God, the unworthy creature before the almighty and all-loving Creator. Its physical expression (and for the Hebrews many attitudes of worship were based on physical postures) is that of kneeling. The Syrophoenician woman, finding Jesus, 'fell at his feet' (Mark 7:25). I have come across the same thing in my travels in Asia; men and women alike who have been healed of deafness, blindness or some crippling disorder have come afterwards to kiss my feet in a gesture of humble thanksgiving. Of course it was God who healed them, not me, but the posture they adopt to express their feelings is one with which we are familiar. Humility is pleading to God, who 'resisteth the proud, but giveth grace to the humble' (Jam. 4:6). Not only that, it is the humble whose prayers are most readily answered. 'If my people shall humble themselves, and pray,' God said to Solomon, 'then I will hear from heaven . . . ' (2 Chr. 7:14). Our status as children of God does not permit us to take liberties; humility belongs to our origins as outsiders to the grace of God, and it is to be retained in our bearing as Christians. Anything else is unbecoming. The late Poet Laureate John Betjeman, asked to assess his own work, replied 'I don't think I am any good, and if I thought I was any good, I wouldn't be any good.'

Adopting a right attitude to God – something we all too easily lose in the desperation to have our prayers answered – is the point where receiving begins. Faithful trust in the love of God, linked with a proper humility in worship before him, will bring us out of the forest of confusion into a clearing where the sky above is open and we can get our bearings. When the woman, at the feet of her Saviour, gave that response which indicated her right attitude to God, Jesus replied '*For this saying* go thy way . . .' (italics mine) and she received the miracle she had been looking for. 'When she was come to her house, she found the devil gone out, and her daughter laid upon the bed' (Mark 7:30).

But she received two other things as well, and these in a way were more wonderful. One was the commendation of Jesus, the reassurance that she was spiritually in tune with God. In comparison to this even the most amazing healings are insignificant. As Kathryn Khulman said, 'If I never see another miracle, as long as I see people born again, I see the great miracle and I am satisfied.' A miracle is a temporary work of God; the great miracle of salvation is the highest prize, the richest reward, and lasts forever.

In addition to, and perhaps because of that, the woman obtained peace of mind. In the words of the hymn:

'O what peace my Saviour gives
Peace I never knew before;
For my way has brighter grown
Since I learned to trust him more.'

The famous British Prime Minister William Gladstone once attributed his great calmness to a text displayed on his bedroom wall; it was Isaiah 26:3 – 'Thou wilt keep him in perfect peace, whose mind is stayed on thee.' This was the intention of Jesus, who after his address at the Last Supper told his disciples, 'These things I have spoken unto you, that in me ye might have peace,' (John 16:33) something that Paul echoed when instructing the Colossians, 'Let the peace of God rule in your hearts' (Col. 3:15). The whole world yearns for peace, yet fear and suspicion prevent peace between nations, and anxiety and suffering often keep it far from the individual heart. 'Lord, give us the vision in spite of our human failures,' prayed the astronaut Frank Borman from beyond the moon, 'and the faith to believe for universal peace . . . '

That peace came to the Syrophoenician woman, who had felt the silence of God and come through her distress to a point where in humility she was able to receive from God. It came in the end to the lady I tried in vain to counsel. It is possible for all of us.

12: Sacred Power

In the day when I cried thou answerdst me.

Psalm 138:3

In considering the silences of God we have already moved on to the topic of prayer, for prayer is really our whole communication with God. The problem is this communication is limited, and when we are under stress it can become very limited indeed. A man with a gastric ulcer may be able to think of nothing beyond his own intestines, with the result that his prayer takes on a desperate, clutching quality, like banging the counter bell when there's no one serving in a shop. In itself this kind of prayer is proper and good; it recognises a need of God and looks to him to provide. But urgent, self-motivated petitionary prayer will be insufficient on its own to hold up the extensive superstructure of a man's relationship with God. I'm sure we all have a friend or relative of whom we say, 'The only time we ever hear from him is when he wants something!' In such a case we feel slightly resentful that the person concerned cares less about us than about the favour he hopes we'll give him. God never feels resentment, but he must get an awful lot of *gimme* prayers from people who before that haven't even left him a calling card!

Man's relationship with God has often been compared to a marriage, and this is helpful to our thinking about prayer because the loving husband will do more than make requests of his wife: he will remember to say thanks, and spend time talking, joking, sharing and commiserating with her as the occasion demands. The relationship is dynamic and flexible. Communication may often involve requests, but it is many-sided and built on a mutual commitment without which all contact will remain superficial. Prayer, then, isn't like buying a bag of groceries at the till in Sainsburys. Nor is it like a phone call to a far-away relative – though the telephone is sometimes used as an analogy for prayer. Prayer isn't even like friendship, for it goes far, far deeper than that, deeper even than marriage, which is the best human parallel for a man's relationship with God. But if that's what prayer isn't what *is* it? Paul wrote to the Philippian church, 'Be careful for nothing; but in everything by prayer and supplication with thanksgiving let your requests be made known unto God' (Phil. 4:6). This quotation emphasises the variety of prayer. But it also exposes its very nature, because the expression translated 'unto God' – *pros ton theon*, in the Greek – is identical with that used by John in the first sentence of his Gospel: 'In the beginning was the Word, and the Word was *with God*.' Knox renders it 'abiding with God! So Paul's advice that Christians should let their requests be made known is not an invitation to write in sending a self-addressed envelope; it carries overtones of entry into the very habitation of God, of a constant visiting of heaven to share with God and let him know their needs.

There's no catch. It isn't an underhand way of making people adopt the externals of Christianity. Romance grows as a man and a woman get to know one another, as they learn to communicate; Christian faith grows as they spend time in prayer with their Lord and Creator. You can recognise someone who really prays by the quality of his life – the way he is blessed and achieves his goals, the way his character, motives, morals and actions all bear the unmistakeable stamp of the Master. One of the first things the enemies of the early Christians noticed about them was that they had been with Jesus. They had spent three years in the company of Christ before the crucifixion, and after he ascended to the Father they went on being with him in prayer. The depth of this communication with God was revealed in the miracles they performed and the type of lives they led – you only have to read the book of Acts, for instance, to be amazed at what Paul managed to do during his lifetime, and come to that the equanimity with which he faced his own impending death. There is no doubt that prayer produces supreme quality of character, and the more prayer you do, the more patience and concentration you pour into it, the finer that quality will be.

But prayer also counts towards the ministry of healing. Though I take my own personal prayer very, very seriously, I am under no illusions when it comes to the source of power in my ministry. Yes, I have to put myself in a position of receiving before God that I may pass his gift on to others; but much of the power is 'generated' through faithful Christians who pray sometimes in two or three all-night sessions before a campaign, and then go on praying while I preach. I can often sense between eight-thirty and nine o'clock a peaking of spiritual power which I know in my spirit is a consequence of prayer being offered in a small side room. That is why I value other believers' prayer so highly. I was greatly humbled and encouraged a few years ago to meet a minister who had heard me speak ten years before on my need for prayer, and had prayed for me every day since!

Prayer, then, is a vital issue in the ministry of healing, and for that reason I am devoting a chapter to it in this book. But I am aware also that, as Spurgeon said, 'Prayer is an art which only the Holy Ghost can teach us . . . ' There is no simple ABC I can give you about prayer any more than I could develop a technique for falling in love. Prayer gives us an awesome glimpse into the love of the Almighty; it packs us full of divine chemistry that under the igniting spark of the Spirit will cure the ill and free the oppressed. But nowhere in the teaching of prayer is there a little arrow telling us to light the blue touch-paper and stand well back. I have no formulae. All I can do is pass on a few of the lessons I have learned, and hope that they are sound enough directions to get you further along the road.

We have already noticed how readily we complain, how adept we are at finding fault and blaming others, and how negative and destructive this whole cycle becomes. Well, one sure antidote to it is *thanking God*: '. . . with thanksgiving let your requests be made known unto God,' wrote Paul. Don't slouch up to the altar with a long face and moan about those awful kids next door who stick chewing gum on your fence posts – instead, thank God for the letter that arrived today from a friend you hadn't heard from for months. Don't grouse about the weather – give thanks for the plentiful supply of drinking water that millions have to go without. Don't make a to-do over your husband's clumsiness and lack of consideration – be thankful that he takes the kids out to a football match and brought you a cup of tea in bed last Sunday morning. This isn't pretending that bad things are really good; it's looking for those genuinely good things in life that however few and far between help us to get through the day and enjoy it a little more. Seek them out, cherish them, and when you begin to pray, bring them to mind and give God thanks for them. 'The man who has forgotten to be thankful,' wrote Robert Louis Stevenson, 'has fallen asleep.' He might have said that when a man fills his prayers with complaining, God falls asleep.

Because thanksgiving recognises the hand of God behind all the varied circumstances of life, it leads on naturally to *praising and exalting God*. A telescope is an ingenious device, but the astronomer taking one out on a warm, clear summer evening soon forgets the merits of the instrument as he gazes through it to the real object of his interest – the stars. In the same way the praying Christian, thankful for God's blessing on him in the events of his life, soon sees through those events to God himself, and becomes caught up in praise. And just as with the aid of his telescope the astronomer learns about the night sky and the universe it reveals, praise makes clearer to the human spirit the greatness of the creator. Often in my meetings the atmosphere becomes charged with praise and I can sense the enemy withdrawing like a couger from a forest fire. It is then that I feel able to contend against sickness, trouble and depression, working under the cover of God's protection that praise brings so near. Blessings come down and miracles are abundant. And the same will happen in private prayer; if you worship Jesus with all your heart, if you heap up thanksgiving and praise, you will put him in his rightful place as your Lord and all the coldness and formality will drain away, bringing blessings down on your soul.

But what about asking, or petitionary prayer? Well, imagine a little girl going into a sweet shop. She's about three feet high and barely reaches the top of the counter, so the sales assistant can only see her big eyes ogling at the sweets, and the top of her head, which is slightly damp because it's raining outside. The rest of her body is a blue blur of raincoat through the glass counter. 'What would you like?' asks the assistant, who, being a grandmother, is a sucker for anything in a junior school uniform. 'A sweetie,' the little girl replies. 'Yes, and what sort of sweetie would you like?' There is a long silence; the little girl has her finger in her mouth and is gazing back and forth along the racks of confectionery. Finally it settles on a box of *Lindt* sherry liqueurs . . . 'What about a nice pack of jelly beans?' says the assistant, helpfully, and then holding up a sherbert tube, 'Or what about this?' The little girl shakes her head, but it isn't because she prefers liqueurs – she doesn't know what she wants. The assistant plumps for the jelly beans. 'There we are. I'm sure you'll like these. Now how much money have you got?' A damp hand relaxes its grasp on a single silver coin – five pence – and holds it up for inspection. It will buy precisely three and a half jelly beans, out of a packet of twenty-four, all sealed up in a plastic wrapper. They go back on the rack. 'Why didn't you tell me you only had five pence?' The little girl giggles, and the sales assistant, mindful of three other customers who want evening papers and have trains to catch, exchanges the silver coin for a smaller, copper one and gives the girl a chocolate bar. 'Do you have it in change?' she says to the man with a *Standard* and a five pound note, watching the little girl go out and wondering if that was, after all, what she really wanted.

'It seems,' wrote John Wesley, 'that God is limited by our prayer life. He can do nothing unless someone asks him.' One of the most fundamental principles of petitionary prayer is to *ask clearly*. You don't have to use a megaphone to pray, for God will always hear the prayer of faith, but you do need to say precisely what it is you want. The sales assistant was ready to give out whatever the child's money could pay for – but she didn't know what she wanted. And half the time I'm sure God doesn't know what we want. We pray vaguely for 'blessing' or for God to be 'with someone' when we would do better to decide what we want, state it categorically, and, in the American phrase, *go for it*! Make your order clearly in the restaurant of God's provision and you'll get the feast you're looking for – on the house.

But there is one more, vital point to remember about asking in prayer, and I'll illustrate it with another story.

There was at the time of King Arthur a little-known knight by the name of Sir John Earwigg. Unlike Lancelot, Bors and Galahad he was not terribly famous. Not having slain many dragons or rescued many desperate maidens from dark towers, he didn't qualify for a place at the legendary Round Table, and in fact at dinner time in Camelot he ate from a small square one, facing the wall. But fate was about to single out John Earwigg, for one evening during what was called the Silly Season, when knights went out looking for gallant deeds to perform and left Camelot rather empty, King Arthur needed to deliver a message to a neighbouring earl at Brindthorpe. The King looked to right and left across the empty places of the Round Table and eventually spied Sir Earwigg sitting in the corner.

'You!' he said.

John Earwigg almost swallowed his leg of mutton whole, he was so surprised. He laid his sword on his plate (he always used it to cut the meat when it was tough) and stood up. The king was eyeing him.

'Ever been to Brindthorpe?'

'No, Sire. I think my aunt went once . . . '

'Is she here?'

'No.'

'You'll have to do then. Nice little seaside castle, just your sort of thing. What was your name again?'

'Sir John Earwigg.'

King Arthur had clearly never heard of him before, or if he had he'd long forgotten. Sir John Earwigg was a very forgettable person.

'Splendid,' said the king, producing a long manilla envelope. 'Get on your horse and take this to Brindthorpe for tomorrow morning.'

Earwigg didn't tell the king he'd mortgaged his horse; but then the king hadn't told Earwigg that Brindthorpe lay two hundred miles away across an all but impenetrable forest full of goblins, wicked witches and haunted transport cafés. In the end he persuaded the stable boy to give him an old grey cart-horse called Twinkle, and set off southwards with his second-hand suit of armour and bantam weight lance. He actually had a good many adventures on the way which do not concern us here and which anyway nobody believed when he got back. At the end of the week he rounded a hill to see Brindthorpe Castle ahead of him.

The drawbridge was pulled up fast. Sir Earwigg gazed at the black water and the sheer walls behind it.

'Ahoy there!' he shouted.

There was a short scuffling sound – the kind a person makes when he is dropping a newspaper and getting up in a hurry – and a nose appeared in the narrow window by the portcullis.

'Whad'ya want?' it said.

'I have a message for the Earl of Brindthorpe. Open up!'

'What sorta' message?'

'A message. Just a message.'

'What's it say?'

'How do I know? Open up, you fool!'

'If you're sellin' brushes I can tell you right now the Earl don't want none.'

'I am not selling brushes!'

'The milkman's already been, an' the fishmonger comes on Chewsdays.'

'Do I look as if I'd sell anyone fish?'

The nose momentarily vanished. 'Blimey, Sid, this one's a right banana,' it said over its shoulder.

At that moment a wave of knightly dignity, heightened by the week's valiant exploits, surged in Earwigg's veins and he cried, 'Open up in the name of Sir John Earwigg!'

There was a short pause. Then a stifled snort. Then another shorter pause. Then the noses – it sounded like fifty of them – broke out in guffaws of laughter.

Sir John Earwigg was shattered. He had not known humiliation like this since Lancelot, mistaking him for a dustbin, had lifted up his visor and stuffed a bucketful of vegetable peelings into his breastplate. And at least Lancelot had been drunk.

'You'll pay for this,' he snarled, but the noses only began laughing again because Twinkle had got bored and was casually pulling up dandelions. Sir John Earwigg lowered his head in shame – and then an idea came to him. After all, he wasn't here on his own business; he couldn't care less about getting into their measly castle. He was here simply because King Arthur had sent him. He drew a deep breath. 'Open up in the name of the king!'

The laughter stopped, and the nose was once again inserted through the window.

'What king?'

'King Arthur. I am bringing a message from King Arthur!'

'You ain't pullin' my leg?'

'Open up!'

'Blimey!' said the nose, amid sounds that resembled the winding of a huge grandfather clock, 'we're gonna be for it if the guv'ner 'ears about this . . . '

Trotting over the drawbridge Sir John Earwigg allowed himself a faint smile.

End of story. Before you read any further you might like to test yourself by guessing what its moral is! What in fact I meant to show is that all asking takes place within an authority structure, and where the asking person stands in that structure will decide what answer he gets. As an individual – particularly one with such an unfortunate name – John Earwigg could not persuade the guards to lower the drawbridge; but as an envoy of the king he was immediately recognised and accepted. He came in the *name* of the king. Now all that didn't disappear with the Middle Ages. You wouldn't take any notice of the tax inspector if his letters didn't come in the name of the government – *On Her Majesty's Service*, as the envelope makes quite clear. You might be tempted to defy a policeman were it not for the weight of the courts and the system of law enforcement that stands behind him. It is not the man, but the name in which he comes.

So it is with prayer. In the world of the spirit the name that carries the very highest authority is the name of Jesus: 'God hath . . . given him a name which is above every name: that at the name of Jesus every knee should bow, of things in heaven, and things in earth, and things under the earth; and that every tongue should confess that Jesus Christ is Lord, to the glory of God the Father' (Phil. 2.9–11). It is that name, not ours, that gets things done in heaven. That is why Jesus promised his disciples, 'Whatsoever ye shall ask in my name, that will I do,' (John 14:13) and why when Peter and John met the lame man in the gate of the temple they said to him, 'In the name of Jesus Christ of Nazareth rise up and walk' (Acts 3:6). 'His name through faith in his name hath made this man strong . . . ' they explained later before the Pharisees. The name was the authority in which the healing took place, and it was in that authority Peter and John put their faith. Like Sir John Earwigg they used the name of the king.

The name of Jesus makes small men big. In a way, the tax collector Zaccaeus, who was 'little of stature' (Luke 19:3), was made big by the privilege of his office. But his position was a precarious one, depending as it did on the goodwill of a Roman elite who could only have despised him. He extorted money from his own countrymen in the name of Caesar, while he himself had no hope of attaining Roman citizenship. In Christianity it is different. We are identified with the Lord whose name we use, and so not only have the authority of his name but actually grow ourselves 'unto a perfect man, unto the measure of the stature of the fulness of Christ' (Eph. 4:13). The Puritans knew that the name of Jesus went beyond petitionary prayer; for them it was also 'joy to the heart, honey to the mind and music to the lips . . . ' As we *use the name of Jesus* in our prayers, and *adore the name of Jesus* in our praise, so we will be built up and see miracles happen.

But the sacred power does not only come through the minutes we spend on our knees in prayer. Our prayers will be in vain unless they are backed up with an obedient life, for the *yes* we gave to the Lord at the moment of conversion was not the final statement of our salvation but the start of a whole new lifestyle in which we listen to the promptings of the Spirit and are ready to say yes again and again. The instructions of Jesus' mother Mary to the servants at the marriage feast in Cana is apt for all his followers: 'Whatsoever he saith unto you, do it' (John 2:5). God looks for a broken spirit, that is, one that has no confidence in its own abilities but looks constantly to God for inspiration, strength and guidance. I once heard Corrie ten Boom summarise God's calling like this: 'There is only one way forward in the victorious Christian life–surrender, surrender, surrender; obey, obey, obey!' It is a lesson we should take to heart. In the opinion of the writer on renewal, Jim Wallis, 'the tragedy of modern evangelism is in calling many to believe but few to obey . . . we must stress the rule of God and call people to radical obedience . . . '

Only *radical obedience* will really change things, because that alone releases the sacred power which produces new calls and new opportunities to obey. It was when David Wilkerson gave himself up to God's will in long periods of prayer that he was moved by a newspaper article to live among the delinquent teenagers of New York, and so to found Teen Challenge. It was radical obedience that caused Martin Luther to go out and shake Europe, Jonathan Edwards to start his revivals, John Wesley to mount his horse and through fifty years of tireless evangelism save the nation of England.

Once again I can only affirm this in my own experience. Sacred power is ours through obedient living and faithful prayer, through nothing less, in fact, than a total giving of our lives to God that he may give the fulness of his Spirit to us, and so work miracles among us. Nothing else will do. There are no cheap miracles. God has promised the riches of his power to us on condition that we live faithfully and communicate openly with him, in a way of which marriage is a pale imitation. The Danish philosopher Soren Kierkegaard was right when he said, 'It is hard to believe because it is hard to obey . . . prayer is a silent surrendering of ourselves and everything to God.'

13: Secrets of a Supernatural Ministry

My speech . . . was not with enticing words or man's wisdom, but in demonstration of the Spirit and of power . . .

St Paul

There is one question I am nearly always asked when I visit a Bible college or ministerial conference.

It came most recently at a dinner for church leaders in Malaysia. As usual I was observing local custom by eating with chopsticks, and as usual my efforts were being greeted with discreet amusement by everyone present.

'I'm getting quite proficient with these,' I said to the young man on my left. In Britain he would have passed as a teenager, though I reckoned he must be twenty or twenty-two. Like many pastors in the country he was fresh from college, just beginning his ministry, and eager to learn. To him I must have seemed a virtual patriarch – which is perhaps why he asked the question.

'You have been an evangelist for a long time, Pastor Banks,' he said. 'You have seen many healings. Can you tell me – what is the secret of a miracle ministry?'

I nodded. A moment like that deserves to be savoured, because one is poised to deliver to untried youth all the accumulated wisdom of age and experience. Unfortunately, it is also the moment when the pork ball on the end of your chopsticks comes loose and falls heavily into a bowl of sweet and sour sauce. The thick red liquid jumps out in all directions, coating the table and making a dramatic arrival on your tie.

So much for age and experience. Truly, I thought, this treasure is contained in earthen vessels.

I laid the chopsticks down with a sigh and asked my host for a spoon. The pause did at least give me a moment to consider my reply, and when I had made it I went on thinking about the matter for quite some time. I have been in evangelism for twenty years now. I can look back on thirty-seven pioneer churches, countless healings and innumerable conversions – some of the men converted in my early campaigns are now elders and pastors in their own right. If there are any 'secrets' involved, they have to do with my whole lifestyle, and that is hard to take apart and analyse. Not only that; these secrets aren't things which I have done in the past and may consequently forget about in the present. I am just as deficient in many respects as I ever was, and if I am able to put my finger on the secrets of success it is in the knowledge that I myself have a lot of work left to do.

Here then, are given very open secrets about the healing ministry:

The first secret: *Quietness and waiting*

'Everywhere today,' wrote G. K. Chesterton, 'there is noise, bustle and confusion, but nowhere quiet hearts.'

That was over fifty years ago. How many things have worsened since then can be judged by a trip to the cinema. Modern thrillers, with their constant action, fast cutting, hard-hitting sound effects and fluid plots, have made their older counterparts look cumbersome and dated. Speed is now part of our consciousness, part of our expectation of life. The Atlantic crossing that took four days by ship now takes a mere four hours in a plane, and as speed of movement has increased so too has our need for perpetual activity, work and amusement. We live as well as drive in the fast lane, with less and less time for reflection about where exactly we are headed or the morality we take with us. In Aaron Linford's words: 'We are carried along in the stampede of confused emotions and blunted principles . . . '

Now against that the references in Scripture to rest and quietness: 'Better is a handful with quietness, than both the hands full with travail and vexation of spirit' (Eccles. 4:6). 'In quietness and confidence shall be your strength' (Isa. 30:15). 'Be still, and know that I am God' (Psa. 46:10). 'Study to be quiet . . . ' (1 Thess. 4:11). Certainly, Christians have found that at the moments of greatest trial it is in stillness before God that strength has come. Edith Cavell, a heroine of the First World War, wrote shortly before her death, 'Here shall thy shelter be, in my arms my dear; the sun shall come back to thee . . . resting, relaxing in him.' It seems that God calls his people, not to the frenetic hustle of modern life, but to an inner tranquility cultivated by waiting in his presence. As Robert Louis Stevenson said, 'Quiet minds cannot be perplexed, but go on . . . like a clock in a thunderstorm.'

The problem is, evangelical Christians have the idea that in the race of life anything less than full throttle is an insult to God. In one way that is true – we are called to be faithful workers for the Kingdom, and not lazy slackers. But that leaves open the question exactly what this work consists of. We all too easily identify working for the Kingdom with the ceaseless clamour of activity in the world, so that conversion only changes us from worldly workaholics into spiritual ones. Yet what is really required is a transformation not just of the object of our exertions, but of the way in which we go about them. In the words of Bernard of Clairvaux, 'Waiting upon God is not idleness, but work which beats all other work.'

A little meditation on the word of God shows this to be true. At the end of the day Jesus often 'sent the multitudes away' and 'went up into a mountain apart to pray: and when the evening was come, he was there alone' (Matt. 14:23). He wasn't perpetually ministering – he took time for deep spiritual refreshment in the presence of his Father. Remember as well the marvellous passage in the Old Testament where Elijah, struck by a fit of depression after his victory on Mount Carmel, hides away in a cave. 'A great and strong wind rent the mountains, and break in pieces the rocks before the Lord; but the Lord was not in the wind:

and after the wind an earthquake, but the Lord was not in the earthquake; and after the earthquake a fire, but the Lord was not in the fire.' And after the fire? A *still small voice*. Quietness in the presence of God, that gave Elijah the strength to complete his mission.

Quietness and waiting have two good effects. One is that our souls are set free from the frantic wind of activity and drift down like feathers into rest. We find out roots, move to the centre of the spinning disc where there is no motion. This in itself will be of enormous benefit; in Pascal's words, 'All men's miseries derive from not being able to sit quietly in a room alone.' But there is more. The second good effect of quietness is that we are able to hear sounds previously drowned out. Sitting in Pascal's quiet room we are not quite alone, but in the presence of God as Jesus was – not praising, not making a great fuss or sweating drops of blood, but just sitting and listening. Anything God says to us in the myriad different ways he speaks is more valuable than the torrent of words we pour out when we normally come to prayer.

No meeting with God can leave us unchanged, and a meeting at depth will change us profoundly. If we don't come out like Moses with our faces shining, then the change will show in other ways, in the steadied rhythm of our lives or the greater tranquility of our souls. John Wesley knew that well, for as one of the busiest and most successful of preachers he was able to say, 'I am always in haste, but never in a hurry.' And I believe we will be most fruitful, will preach most effectively and see the greatest signs and wonders, when we are imbued with the peace, certainty and confidence that come from quietness and waiting before God.

'Drop thy still dews of quietness
Till all our striving cease;
Take from our souls the strain and stress,
And let our ordered lives confess
The beauty of thy peace.'

The second secret: *Set definite objectives.*

We must not be merely dreamers. The gospel singer Mahalia Jackson once gave young people this advice: 'Ask yourself, "What do I want to be? Where do I want to go?" God will lift you up. But there is one condition – *you have got to have made up your mind!*'

Setting objectives and sticking to them takes a stoutness of heart that comes only by seeking God until we have the positive assurance of his calling. For me that moment came with the unexpected success of my crusade at Horncastle. I knew then that a ministry in healing and evangelism was possible, and decided to try it out and see how the Lord would lead me. Within three years it was confirmed by the tremendous revival at Wigan. I remember committing myself from that moment to bring the full gospel to a lost world, and healing to a pain-ridden, paralysed, sick depressed and broken humanity. When not long ago I returned to Wigan and four thousand people turned out to the rugby ground on a ferociously windy day to hear the gospel, the Senior Minister Ray Belfield whispered to me, 'It's amazing what prayer and faith will do when you have a definite *goal*!' As it happened we were sitting right over the goal line.

Often the difference between success and failure is our willingness to ignore uncertainty and put our best foot forward. 'He who has a firm will moulds the world to himself,' said Goethe. And even if our will isn't as firm as we'd like, we can pray with diligence for strength to do what by nature comes to us with great difficulty. 'Assume a virtue if you have it not,' advised Shakespeare in *Hamlet*. Assuming, claiming what is really ours, brings victory and overcomes the Evil One. Nor should we be discouraged if we think God is calling us to do the impossible. Mrs Yonggi Cho was very nervous about her husband's plan to build a five thousand seater church in Seoul – he had no money, for a start, and they lived in an old flat with so many mice in the floorboards tht the whole place rattled and squeaked. One night she lay awake listening to them and said, 'If it's your will, God, to build this huge church and do this impossible task, please stop those mice right now!' In a matter of seconds the noise stopped, and it never came back. And Seoul now has a church holding many more than ten thousand people.

God has never failed to meet the goals I have set over the twenty years of my ministry, and I can think of no better weay of summing the point up than to quote a few little proverbs about goals from the American pastor Jim Williams. So remember:

'Every goal is a statement of faith.
If you fail to plan, you are planning to fail.
He who aims at nothing is sure to hit it,
It is better to attempt something and fail, than to
attempt nothing and succeed.'

The third secret: *Keep in God's love.*

There is no more eloquent comment on the theory of divine love than Paul's in 1 Corinthians 13, and no more perfect example of its practice than the life of Christ recorded in the Gospels. Both repay regular study. But it is important to realise that love is more than what God does, or what Christ did, or what Christians are supposed to do. It is the cutting edge of the kingdom, the quality without which a thousand healings will be mere sensation and all preaching sophistry and cant. We must be soaked in the love of God. Love alone will keep us tender and sweet in the bitterness of life's experience and destroy our enemies by loving them into friends.

Love goes beyond generous sentiments. It will often demand sacrifice. 'Love,' said David Watson, 'is turning a blind eye and a deaf ear to the faults and failings of others . . . always making peace, being positive, believing the best about others, not fearing the worst. It is always upbuilding.' David Watson lived what he taught. With only a few weeks left to live he wrote to all the Christian brothers he felt could have misunderstood him, to make amends and reassure them of his *love*. Here was a man bathed in the graciousness of his Master, full of humility and tenderness in the time of trial, showing the love of God so completely that the thought of it has sometimes moved me to tears. And so it should, for we cannot help but be touched by the power of divine love. It is able to preach the gospel in places words cannot reach and where miracles fail. Said William Barclay, 'More people have been brought into the church by the kindness of real Christian love . . . it can break the hardest and cruellest heart. It is steadfast in the very worst of storms.' Not long ago I saw a newspaper article which illustrated this very well. It reported a party held for an eighty-year-old woman who before the last war had gone to teach in the poverty-stricken inner city. In the area where she lived, it said, the crime rate among young people had fallen dramatically; and in fact many of the birthday guests, among whom were doctors, lawyers and even one cabinet minister, had once been her pupils. What was the secret of her success? 'I don't know,' she replied. 'When I look at modern teachers and their methods, I feel so ill prepared to teach . . . ' And then she added, 'I had nothing to give but love.' Naturally, that was the best of all.

Miracles thrive on our love for others. If we want to have a life and ministry blessed with the gift of healing, we must *love*; we must make it our theme. The Victorian writer Charles Kingsley wrote on his wife's gravestone three Latin words: *Amavimua, amamis, amabimus. We have loved, we love, we shall always love.* We could do a lot worse than to have the same message engraved on our hearts.

The fourth secret: *Have simple faith.*

We have already seen how important faith is in the process of divine healing. But faith is not a spur-of-the-moment necessity for calling down the healing power of the Spirit; for the man or woman in the healing ministry it is something to be lived day by day. This is the sort of faith Jesus called for: 'Nevertheless when the Son of man cometh, shall he find faith on the earth?' (Luke 18:8). As Shakespeare reminded his audience in the *Winter's Tale*, 'It is required of you to awake your faith . . . '

Fundamentally faith is exercised in God himself. 'Who is he that overcometh the world,' asked John, 'but he that believeth that Jesus is the Son of God? (1 John 5:5). Yet so close are God and his word that we cannot believe in one without also believing in the other. According to Samuel Chadwick, 'Faith is built on knowledge of God's word.' The word embodies *the Word*, so that Paul described the gospel, the good news about Jesus, as 'the word of faith, which we preach' (Rom. 10:8). And when in the next verse he went on to say ' . . . if thou shalt . . . believe in thine heart that God hath raised him from the dead, thou shalt be saved,' it is clear that his believing in God takes for granted another kind of believing in Paul's preaching. 'How shall they believe in him of whom they have not heard? And how shall they hear without a preacher? . . . So then faith cometh by hearing, and hearing by the word of God' (Rom 10:14, 17).

This will mean believing what the Bible says, since the Bible is the most reliable preacher. If the Bible asks us to accept the virgin birth, the resurrection, the ascension and Pentecost as historical facts then we must lay our doubts aside and believe. Nothing will come, anyway, of hanging on to reservations which we can never prove and which themselves grow out of modern society's chronic cynicism. I believe without reservation these great biblical facts.

The other vital thing about faith is that it must be put into practice. Like muscle, unused it quickly turns into flab – which is more or less what James meant by saying that faith without works is dead. In a service for the poor held many years ago in a tiny Rumanian church, a conspicuous absentee was the local farmer. But just as people were saying to one another how uncaring this wealthy man was not to come and pray with them, his son appeared – with several large sacks of wheat. 'This is my father's prayer,' he said. Faith is more than believing. It's *doing* what God wants you to do, and *being* what God wants you to be; as Billy Graham put it, 'Letting go and relying entirely on God.' That may be a lot more risky than giving away a few sacks of grain from your granaries, and it is at this pont that we discover what being a Christian is really all about, since, in the words of T. L. Osborn, 'Faith moves the hand of God, and the hand of God moves everything else.' We have a God who is able to work wonders if only we will give him sufficient room within our faith. We do not have to accept defeat when everybody else says a situation is hopeless, because God will gain a foothold on our faith even if it is only as big as a mustard seed, and on that leverage he can toss mountains into the sea. Of course, he may leave it till the very last moment, as I well know after twenty years of evangelistic ministry; but he certainly never fails. He honours the faith of those who serve him. On at least one occasion I have felt it right to mortgage my house to support a campaign. My wife and I have in material terms risked all that we own because of our overriding and God-given love for the sick and lost. At these times no churches or denominational committees would put up the money, and yet we knew absolutely that the crusade had to go ahead. Had it failed we would have been made bankrupt overnight – but God is faithful; we did not go without, and in those towns where we were called on to exercise this faith there are strong, new churches.

We must have faith in the same style as that of Martha, whose trust in Jesus was complete even on the death of her brother. When Mary was immobilised by grief she came forward to meet the Saviour. 'But I know that even now whatsoever thou wilt ask of God, God wilt give it thee' (John 11:22). She had faith for a miracle.

The fifth secret: *Leave one foot in the world.*

Christians are awfully clannish. Put them together and they will form impenetrable groups, write new choruses, refine their worship with electronics and spiritual gifts, and develop their own incomprehensible jargon about sins, salvation, shepherding, covering and discipling. Very often, in fact, they cease to be fishermen and become fishmongers instead.

'We must visit hell in our imagination,' said the great William Booth, founder of the Salvation Army. All the business of church life is necessary and important, but as soon as it takes priority over contacts with the world the Christian church loses its relevance. 'Keep your hand on the pulse beat of the world,' Billy Richards advised me years ago, and how right he was. If we are to evangelise effectively we must know the people outside our Christian clique and what sort of world they live in. We may be surprised at the opportunities we have been passing up. A recent pop song, for instance, includes these lines:

'I woke up today, I was crying,
Lost in a lost world, so many people are dying.
Lost in a lost world,
O can you feel the world is pining,
Pining for someone who really cares?'

For me, the greatest prize for the pastor, evangelist or believer is the one named in Daniel: 'They that turn many to righteousness (shall shine) as stars for ever and ever' (Dan. 12:3). It is too easy to lose ourselves in the comforts of Christian fellowship. We should be out in the world, befriending and living alongside those we usually neglect in order to make time for another church meeting–colleagues at work, young people, members of ethnic minorities, even our own families. God has a long reach. I have seen many Moslems converted at recent crusades, and they are often regarded as the hardest to win for the gospel. The fact is that every man, woman and child is in need of God, and many of them, like the song writer quoted above, know it all too well. We must feel their sadness, weep with them, be one with them in their despair, and let God mediate his power through us to work their salvation. If we are to act as bridges between the world and the Kingdom, we must have a firm grip on both sides of the ravine.

14: Completing the Miracle

I will deliver thee, and thou shalt glorify me.

Psalm 50:15

No miracle is complete in itself. The man who receives healing from God and takes his religious commitment no further is like the patient accepting treatment for his cut finger but not for a broken leg. Because we have spiritual and mental faculties as well as physical, mere bodily healing is never enough. Remember the ten lepers healed on their way to the priest; only one came back, 'and with a loud voice glorified God . . .' and Jesus answering said, "Were there not ten cleansed? But where are the nine?" There are not found that returned to give glory to God, save this stranger. And he said unto him, "Arise, go thy way: they faith hath made thee whole"' (Luke 17:15, 17–19). This tenth leper, a Samaritan, an outsider, received a fuller healing than the other nine because his faith brought him to God as well as ridding him of leprosy.

This completion can be worked out in two ways. The first way is to *glorify God for a healing*. That is the primary purpose of all divine healing, because it puts God in his rightful position as Lord and Saviour and brings men closer to him. 'This sickness is not unto death,' said Jesus of the ailing Lazarus, 'but for the glory of God, that the Son of God might be glorified thereby' (John 11:4). He did not mean that his raising of Lazarus would be a spectacular publicity stunt for the gospel, though it certainly had that spin-off. He wanted men to recognise him for what he was – the Almighty clothed in human flesh. Time and again in the Gospel records of his miracles have this effect. The paralytic unceremoniously lowered at Jesus' feet by his four friends finally 'departed to his own house, glorifying God.' Not only that, but the crowd 'were all amazed, and they glorified God, and were filled with fear . . . ' (Luke 5:25, 26). Everyone ascribed the wonderful healing to the goodness of God; if you like, they gave God his due. It was often a marvellous, almost heady appreciation of his love expressed in Jesus: 'And he laid his hands on her: and immediately she was made straight and glorified God . . . and all the people rejoiced for all the glorious things that were done by him' (Luke 13:13, 17).

Yet a momentary glorification of God is of little use unless it produces lives that through fresh commitment and love bring constant glory to him. We have heard much recently about the need of ongoing financial support for African relief, not just once-off giving; and so it is with our glorification of God. If our ultimate purpose as Christians is to bring God the honour due to his name, then we must keep on bringing it. It isn't an onerous duty laid on us as payment for health; it is our role in creation and a source of unutterable joy. How do we begin? Easy: by *following Jesus* in a life of sincere Christian discipleship, just as the blind man did who, given God's word of healing, 'received his sight, and followed Jesus in the way' (Mark 10:52). And we'll soon find out that healing isn't the only blessing that comes our way in the service of the Lord. As usual, the psalmist hits the nail on the head: 'Bless the Lord . . . who forgiveth all thine iniquities, who healeth all thy diseases; who redeemeth thy life from destruction; who crowneth thee with loving kindness and tender mercies; who satisfieth thy mouth with good things; so that thy youth is renewed like the eagle's' (Psa. 103:2–5).

So if you have come to a crusade or been prayed for by Christians at your local church, and have received any measure of healing from the Lord, make sure you *complete the miracle*. Give glory to God in your heart and in your testimony to others; and follow Jesus by joining in your local Christian fellowship and committing your life day by day to the Lord. If you have never been a Christian before you will probably feel that the miracle of your healing is overshadowed by an even greater miracle – that of your full salvation in Jesus Christ.

Thine be the glory

For preachers, seeing people healed through their ministry is a dangerous thing. Naturally, the crowd at a crusade will be a mixed bunch, and many of them will believe quite sincerely that the miracles are due to the preacher and not to the God he serves. If God is doing the healing, they ask, why do the miracles always happen through this man and not through anyone else? It's a hard question to ignore; miracles do tend to happen with certain individuals, and a healing evangelist will consequently be tempted to think himself a bit out of the common run – in other words, to take some of the glory for himself instead of giving it all to God.

I know how strong this temptation can be. After a meeting in Northamptonshire a few years ago I could not get out of the doors for all the pressmen, and ended up being carried shoulder high like I'd just won the FA Cup. The men who picked me up had received healing themselves, and their action, besides being the only practical way of removing me, was a sign of their thankfulness and respect. None the less I was reminded of the old saying, *It's all right if people praise you, so long as you don't inhale it*. The man inhaling praise, no matter how great his gifts may be, is on the slippery slope – for God will give his glory to no one else. The only kind of glory we should have as Christians is that which we reflect like tiny mirrors from the light of God's own presence. That does not set us up as idols to be revered and respected in God's place, but rather diminishes us, puts us in our proper position beneath his throne. Probably we are unaware of reaching such a state, for it is a gradual melting into the likeness of God which, by the transforming power of the Spirit, allows those around us to glimpse the nature of God. But it is only a glimpse; it does not really belong to us any more than the candle inside it belongs to a Halloween pumpkin. 'But we all, with open face beholding as in a glass the glory of the Lord, are changed into the same image from glory to glory, even as by the Spirit of the Lord' (2 Cor. 3:18). ' . . . therefore glorify God in your body, and in your spirit, which are God's' (1 Cor. 6:20).

To release the glory to God is liberating and empowering. As Selwyn Hughes has put it, 'There is nothing God cannot do if we keep our hands off the glory!' It permits God to work in us our real glory, the likeness of his Son, so that we show his power, wisdom and grace without trying to draw attention to ourselves. After all, as we saw in the first chapter, drawing attention to themselves was the sin that bedevilled Adam and Eve, and got mankind into the big trouble he's in. A shorter name for it is *pride*. Get rid of pride–all desire to be somebody special on your own, independent of God–and you are on the way to becoming that beautiful creature God intended man to be, reflecting like finely polished crystal the light of his countenance. Who wants to be stuck with his own face when he could have a face like God's?

The old Cornish evangelist Billy Bray was nicknamed the Glory Man because he glorified God for everything that happened to him. Not everything that happened was good, either; one autumn he lost his entire potato harvest, which for a country yokel 140 years ago meant poverty and possibly starvation. Billy marched up and down the rows lifting ham after ham–not a potato on any of them. Finally he stopped. He was hearing a little voice whispering in his mind, and one that he knew did not come from the Holy Spirit . . .

'So this is the good God you serve, eh, Billy? Well, the Lord's certainly looked after you this time, hasn't he? No tatties, no food. For the winter!'

At this point Billy stopped listening and roared back in a voice that could be heard in every house for a mile around, 'What are y' talkin' about? A pretty poor service I got from thee all those years I followed thee, Smutty Face! Away with thee!' And then he danced up and down to rows singing, 'Glory, glory, glory, praise the Lord!'

In a few hours' time there arrived on Billy's doorstep a gift from someone who knew nothing at all about his failed harvest. It was enough potatoes to feed him and his large family into the next spring.

About a century later, in the mid fifties, other men and women were giving glory to God. They were a small group of early charismatics shunned by the established pentecostal churches and referred to as the Glory people. They weren't perfect—their services sometimes failed to give due emphasis to the preaching of God's word. But they had a wonderful ability to praise God without inhibition, and they pioneered many forms of worship—like dancing in the Spirit—that have become common in more recent renewal movements. It may be that the members of the group, which disbanded after a few years, acted as leaven to speed up renewal, for many of them are now evangelists, musicians and pastors, and play an important role in the charismatic revival today.

But there is another aspect to glory that we have not yet considered. We give God glory in a number of ways—by heartfelt worship, obedient living, and by acknowledging his power and Lordship. But there are occasions when God gives his glory to *us* in the sense that his presence is manifested in a tangible way. This experience of God's *shekinah* glory was comparatively common during Israel's wanderings in the wilderness. 'And the glory of the Lord filled the tabernacle. And Moses was not able to enter into the tent of the congregation, because the cloud abode thereon, and the glory of the Lord filled the tabernacle . . . ' (Exod. 40:34, 35). The shepherd saw it at the birth of Christ, when 'the angel of the Lord came upon them, and the glory of the Lord shone round about them: and they were sore afraid' (Luke 2:9). So did the disciples Peter and John at the transfiguration: 'his countenance was altered, and his raiment was white and glistering . . . they saw his glory . . . ' (Luke 9:29, 32).

I have experienced something like this on only a few occasions, but the effect of God's glory coming into the midst of his people is illustrated very clearly by a meeting I held in a small chapel in Billy Bray's county of Cornwall. When it came people began weeping all over the room; I felt so weak in the knees that I could hardly stand up, and soon after delivering a short word I was swept off my feet along with everybody else by the magnificent power of God. It was God's glory coming upon us, a radiance and a joy that in more ways than one were completely out of his world. When we got to our feet again an hour later, we were filled with the Holy Spirit, and we sang and danced and even marched out on to the country lanes proclaiming Christ to passers-by just as the early apostles had done at Pentecost. Nor did the glory die away overnight; in the next town we went to my team was accompanied by all those who had experienced the visitation of God, and as a result the subsequent meetings were blessed with extraordinary power. Many miraculous healings occurred, and on one night in the little chapel nearly a hundred people came to Christ.

Another time God's glory came in a visible form. At the end of a meeting at a church in Eastwood, Nottingham, the pastor Ray Graham and a number of others noticed a lovely purple cloud hanging in one corner of the hall. It was about six feet wide by ten feet high, and emanated such a powerful sense of God's presence that many of those who saw it shed tears of joy and godly fear. Long after this glory-cloud had gone the church was filled with a new vitality, and such is the programme or outreach sustained by the congregation that the building has had to be extended.

Finally, I have known God's glory to be mediated not by sights or sounds, or sensations of spiritual power, but by the fragrance of the Spirit. It came down on a meeting in the Isle of Wight, a light smell of indescribable sweetness. Several ladies in the room started looking in their handbags to see if they'd spilt some perfume, but none of them had, and anyway this fragrance was infinitely superior to anything that comes in a bottle. Many of those present at the meeting said later that it had followed them home; at the café one brother visited afterwards the waitress taking his order sniffed and said, 'That's lovely-smelling oil you have on. What on earth is it? He replied, 'It's not from earth at all,' and when she asked what he meant he was able to witness to her about the saving power of Christ. You might say it was a heaven-scent opportunity . . .

Some Christians say that these physical manifestation of God's glory are peripheral to the real business of the Christian life, and in a sense they are right: there are many more things for us to do than bask in the radiant presence of our God. At the same time, though, we should remember that this basking, this worshipful appreciation of God's splendour and majesty, is what we are called to in the coming age. 'Behold,' cried a voice to the Apostle John, 'the tabernacle of God is with men, and he will dwell with them, and they shall be his people, and God himself shall be with them . . . ' (Rev. 21:3). Whether we should understand from the images presented to us here that heaven consists of a vast, glorious city lit by the light of God's presence, is impossible to say. But the intention of the passage is clear – we will be living with God, and compared to that the surges of spiritual power, purple clouds and sweet fragrances are just trailers.

The healing glory

The final night on a recent crusade took a long time to close. After the long healing line had been patiently and lovingly ministered to the congregation broke out in song after song in praise and adoration of the Lord, and it was a while before I found a gap long enough to squeeze in the final prayer.

I sat down to find a scrap of paper thrust into my hand by the local pastor. On it was written an address.

'I said you'd go along to join them before you left town tomorrow, and give thanks for the mission.'

I agreed to go, and the next morning I rolled up outside a tidy suburban house of the sort you can find practically anywhere in England. I didn't know the house, but I remembered the family who lived in it – the wife had attended a meeting a week before, where she miraculously received her sight. As I went in her first grandchild, whom she had never seen before this crusade, was busy showing her a new dress and pointing out the bright red neck tie and frilly cuffs. A lot of other people were there too; neighbours, friends and relatives – a pretty typical cross-section of local society with the one thing in common that they had all recently become Christians. It was funny to observe all these people who only a week before could hardly have known each other, and probably wouldn't have stopped on the street to say hello, now all gathered together in warm Christian fellowship.

We all sat down to worship and glorify God, singing, praying and holding hands with no sense of embarrassment. Many gave thanks for the way Irene's healed vision had become the talk of the town, and through being reported in the newspapers had drawn in people by their hundreds to find salvation in Jesus Christ. It was marvellous, I reflected, how the opening of this woman's eyes had resulted in the opening of so many blind spiritual eyes. All of the men and women in this room had entered into the promised land of God's blessing. As it said in the passage I read out from Leviticus: 'I will give peace in the land, and ye shall lie down, and none shall make you afraid . . . ' (Lev. 26:6).

When it was time to start on the long drive south they all came out to wave me off. It was spitting rain, and climbing into the car I switched on the wipers; they swept back and forth over the glass, smearing the drops of water into a haze. But as it cleared again the haze remained, and I realised my eyes were brimming with tears. The thought had returned to me in another form: 'Ye . . . which in time past were not a people, but are now the people of God: which had not obtained mercy, but now have obtained mercy' (1 Pet. 2:10). How great was the mercy of God, and how marvellous the power he gave his ministers to bring healing to human lives! There was a price to pay: in twenty years of ministry I had been away from my family for weeks and months at a stretch, and I had missed out on many of the joys of seeing my two boys growing up . . . But what a high calling it was, and what an immense privilege to take part in the fulfilling of God's prophecy through Isaiah: 'The eyes of the blind shall be opened, and the ears of the deaf shall be unstopped. Then shall the lame man leap as a heart, and the tongue of the dumb sing: for in the wilderness shall waters break out, and streams in the desert' (Isa. 35:5, 6).

I pressed a button and the window wound down on the passenger side. Leaning over I looked at this batch of newborn souls. All of them were filled with joy. They waved, they sang; the children danced about and Irene smiled at me with those freshly healed eyes. As I pulled away they joined in a chorus that must have summed up their experience in the crusade, and certainly expressed the joy and totality of divine healing:

'Jesus take me as I am
I can come no other way;
Take me deeper into you
Make my flesh life melt away.

Make me like a precious stone
Crystal clear and finely honed;
Life of Jesus shining through
Giving glory back to you.'

It was all worth it, I thought as I drove out on to the road. For these brothers and sisters the biggest secret had been the fact of healing itself. Soon enough they would go on to discover the biblical teaching about miracles, but the greatest and most important discovery had already been made – that God desires to heal his people.

It is that secret, more than any other, that stands at the very centre of my ministry, and it is my chief joy to 'leak' it wherever I go. But are there not further secrets, mysteries beyond those I have been able to explain in this book? Yes, and sometimes they are baffling and hurtful because as a mere human being I cannot see into the perfect ways of the Creator. All I can do is imitate St Francis, who is pictured in the *Little Plays* discussing with Brother Elias the message they are called to bring to fallen man. 'God has told us what we need to know,' he says. 'We must go and tell *that* . . . '

As for all those other secrets, they will be revealed in good time when Jesus returns to complete the healing, not just of his people, but of the whole world.

Healing Revolution

This is Melvin Banks' first book, in which he tells the story of how God led him in a totally unexpected way into a healing ministry.

'It was . . . very exciting reading, and a testimony to the greatness of our Lord Jesus Christ . . . so interesting to sense the tremendous ways of God.'

Clive Calver, General Secretary, Evangelical Alliance

' . . . with its message of deliverance and faith we commend this . . . outstanding ministry . . . ' *Yonggi Cho*

'Highly recommended . . . a tremendous book . . . '

Colin Whittaker, Pastor, Mount of Olives, Bristol

'This inspiring volume further contributes to the vital ministry of evangelism and ultimate revival around the world. It will stimulate and encourage young men to believe God and bring new hope to the broken lives of individuals.'

Ray Belfield, Pastor, Wigan

Ministers and clergy are invited to receive a free copy of this book, by writing with a S.A.E. to the address below. The Rev Banks would also be pleased to hear from readers at the same address:

The Rev. Melvin Banks
Crusade Office
44 Monks Way
Chippenham
Wilts
England.

Tel: 0249–655712.

Healing Revolution can be purchased from Marshalls in bulk orders, at 3, Beggarwood Lane, Basingstoke, Hants; or single copies from your local Bible bookshop or direct from Rev. Melvin Banks' Crusade Office.